How Sweet It Is...
Without the Sugar

Jean C. Wade

Foreword by
Lois Jovanovic, M.D.

CELESTIAL ARTS
Berkeley, California

Note: The information in this book is meant to complement the advice and guidance of your physician, not to replace it. It is very important that people with diabetes, hypoglycemia, and all food allergies have this condition evaluated by a physician. If you are under the care of a physician, you should discuss any major changes in your regimen with him or her. Because this is a book and not a medical consultation, keep in mind that the information presented here may not apply in your particular case. Whenever a question arises, discuss it with your physician.

Many of the designations used by manufacturers and sellers to distinguish their products are claimed as trademarks. Where the publisher is aware of a trademark claim, such designations, in this book, have initial capital letters.

Celestial Arts
P.O. Box 7123
Berkeley, California 94707

Distributed in Canada by Ten Speed Canada, in the United Kingdom and Europe by Airlift Books, in New Zealand by Southern Publishers Group, in Australia by Simon & Schuster Australia, in South Africa by Real Books, and in Singapore, Malaysia, Hong Kong, and Thailand by Berkeley Books.

Library of Congress Card Catalog Number: 99-75825

First printing, 1999
Printed in Canada

1 2 3 4 5 6 7—03 02 01 00 99

*A special someone comes into
the kitchen with his impish eyes and beaming smile.
"Hmmm, you're baking again? Yum yum—more goodies!"
You can't imagine how wonderful this makes me feel.
With all my love, I dedicate this book to my husband David,
who also has diabetes and loves my desserts
"without the sugar."*

CONTENTS

FOREWORD

HOW NICE IT IS to eat dessert again, especially with the luxury of knowing that I am not cheating on my diet! With recipes that range from basic crepes to peanut butter chiffon cheesecake, this cookbook has made my life feel fulfilled—not a simple thing for a person with diabetes. You see, while our bodies may not be able to deal with sugar, most of us find that our appetites don't change so quickly, and we may still crave the finishing touch of a sweet dessert after a meal—particularly when our friends and family seem to be able to eat whatever they like.

Ending a meal with a favorite dessert is something that most people do without even thinking about it, but those of us who don't have normal pancreatic function must either abstain or risk serious health consequences. Research has shown that we must keep our blood sugar levels as normal as possible to prevent complications of diabetes such as eye, kidney, and foot diseases.

Because temptation is all around us, navigating a buffet table or a restaurant menu can still be a minefield, and will remain so until more chefs begin to realize that there are 16 million Americans with diabetes, and many others who need to or choose to limit their sugar intake for various reasons. But despite the trend in restaurants toward sugar-loaded desserts, there's a good reason to celebrate. With *How Sweet It Is...Without the Sugar*, sugar-free desserts made at home can be more delectable than ever before.

Jean Wade's delicious dessert recipes were specifically created to minimize the effect on a diabetic person's blood glucose, and are thus completely free of all sugar, honey, corn syrup, and molasses. As with all good things, however, it is necessary to consume them only in moderation, for these recipes still contain calories and carbohydrates. Too much of a good thing can cause you to gain weight, and can send your blood sugar out of control!

By eating desserts like the ones Jean presents here, and still taking into account the carbohydrate levels of these treats, people with diabetes can enjoy the sweetness without the sin. Enjoy and *bon appetit*!

Lois Jovanovic, M.D.
Director and Chief Scientific Officer, Sansum Medical Research Institute

ACKNOWLEDGMENTS

A BIG THANK YOU TO all my friends and family for the encouragement and steadfast loyalty that I received for so many years while "baking up" this cookbook.

A huge hug for Lois Jovanovic, M.D., who agreed that I should write this cookbook to satisfy the great need for desserts made "without the sugar."

I could not have completed this cookbook without the help of Gerri French, M.S., R.D., who compiled the Nutrition Facts and Diabetic Exchanges for most of the recipes. Joanne Bishop, R.D. compiled the Facts and Exchanges for a portion of them.

Thanks, Jeff. You were one of my best testers, especially since you have no medical need to leave out the sugar. Jeff loves desserts and is the owner of the Summerland Beach Cafe in Summerland, California, where you can find healthy entrees and muffins "without the sugar." He also serves the best coffee!

I would like to give special thanks to each and every person who helped test the recipes, especially the children. Children are the most critical tasters because they will either make faces, take one bite and get rid of it, or ask for more. Kathy, one of my testers who has diabetes, told me that her children enjoyed the Chocolate Chip Cookies so much that they wanted her to bake them for their class party. (When baking for children, though, it's a good idea to use the fructose option in the recipe rather than the artificial sweetener.) I have to admit that I puffed up and patted myself on the back when you all asked for more of your favorite recipes. Of course we all know there were times when changes had to be made. They can't all come out perfect the first time!

I love you, Bill and Janet! Whenever I see my children, it's time to make desserts! We get together with friends and sample a variety of goodies. Then we have constructive comment time. Thanks for all your patience and help.

Teri, thank you so much for setting up the Web page and for extending yourself to do many other favors for me.

Very special thanks go to my good friend and neighbor, Greta, for sampling all of my research.

Last but not least, because you are all so important to me, I want to extend an enormous thank you to everyone at the Sansum Medical Research Institute. As a volunteer in several research trials, I was monitored closely and was able to learn so much about the importance of exercise and diet for people with diabetes. My questions were always answered and explained, and you all seemed to enjoy the dessert tasting sessions. The notes and letters from Sansum's doctors, nurses, clinical research coordinators, secretaries, and dietitian-nutritionist were all so expressive and invigorating. I appreciated all your feedback and finally followed through with that "You should write a cookbook" comment that I heard from all of you. *Merci, c'est finis!*

Introduction

just had to write this dessert cookbook...I did it for all of us who feel shortchanged by the lack of delicious desserts free of those "bad" sugars that our bodies cannot tolerate. These desserts are for everyone—those of us who can't use sugar for medical reasons, as well as for people who simply prefer not to use sugar.

Regardless of your reasons or motivations, this book will provide you with scrumptious, easy-to-make recipes that your family and friends will enjoy. With these recipes, you can maintain a healthy lifestyle and still enjoy delectable desserts. And you'll no longer have to bake versions with and without sugar, because all your guests will be pleased with the sugar-free treats in this book.

If you're like most people, you probably have a sweet tooth and look forward to enjoying delicious desserts. People with no sugar or calorie restrictions are free to pick and choose whatever they want. But sugary desserts are not necessarily a healthy pick. For example, are you aware that one cup of sugar has approximately 800 calories and 200 grams of carbohydrates? Desserts with sugar are therefore highly caloric. I believe that the more sugar you eat, the more you crave, and it becomes almost an addiction. That's why I want to encourage you to give up the sugar.

Sugars and other carbohydrates are the villains that are most likely to cause blood sugar levels to rise. Millions of people live with diabetes, hypoglycemia, and other conditions that demand sugar restrictions. Also, because Type 2 diabetes is increasingly common—and linked to lifestyle factors—many other people are trying to control their weight by eating fewer calories and curbing their intake of sugar.

Desserts are the most difficult recipes to prepare without using granulated or confectioners' sugar, honey, corn syrup, or molasses. Sugar substitutes, natural fruits and juices, all-fruit jellies, and fructose are excellent replacements for sugar. However, we must be careful about how much of these substitutes we add to our recipes, and we have to watch the portion size and quantity that we eat. Figuratively speaking, just because it tastes good, "Don't eat the whole pie."

I've been cooking and baking since the age of seven. Delving into the recipe sections of magazines is one of my favorite pastimes, and a good cookbook library is an absolute necessity. I have a passion for reading cookbooks because I can imagine the taste of a dish as I read the recipe. I also enjoy inventing recipes with different textures and flavors. The recipes in this book were tested for taste and quality, many times over, over a period of three and a half years. The comments were always the same: "If you don't tell anyone that your dessert is made without the sugar, they'll never know it." "Many people think that without the sugar, it can't taste good, but we know better. I want your recipe." "Get that cookbook finished and published!"

I hope that someday it becomes easier to find sugar-free desserts in restaurants. In the meantime, I'm thrilled that my Apple Nut Crisp and Custard Delight have been served on board three Holland America Line cruise ships. The executive chefs told me that there is a big demand for desserts made without the sugar—in fact, they receive hundreds of written requests. This is hardly surprising given the number of Americans who are living with diabetes. Instead of being tempted to cheat on your diet when you go out to eat, try talking to the service staff at your favorite restaurants about your desire for sugar-free desserts. Who knows, you may be able to effect a change that will benefit many people!

My husband and I are among the more than 16 million people with diabetes in the U.S., and as a result, we live with many dietary restrictions. My grandfather, who was a well-known chef in France, had diabetes and died at the age of 42, long before insulin treatment was an option. My mother, also an excellent cook, had Type 2 diabetes and died at 67. I'm sure she would have lived longer had she taken better care of herself by monitoring her diet and her sugar intake. My husband and I are determined to take the best care of ourselves so that we can enjoy longer, healthier lives. I hope all of you will do the same. I know it's tempting to indulge in desserts made with sugar, but you don't have to! Don't cheat—resist temptation and stick to your diet. Remember that your health is at stake. Exercise daily and eat wonderful desserts without the sugar.

I encourage you to try all the recipes in this book before deciding which are your favorites. Everyone ends up with certain ones that they make over and over again for all occasions, and I know you'll find your own "classics" as well. Stay healthy, and please enjoy *How Sweet It Is...Without the Sugar.*

REMEMBER: To prevent bitter-tasting desserts, never bake or boil Equal or NutraSweet.

ABOUT THE FACTS AND EXCHANGES: Ingredients marked as "optional" are included. When the ingredients list offers alternatives (i.e., sugar substitute or fructose), figures are based on the first item listed. Sugar grams are always included in the total carbohydrate counts, in addition to being shown separately.

CHAPTER 1

HINTS, MEASUREMENTS, AND BASICS

Alphabet of Hints and Suggestions

ALWAYS read the recipe thoroughly. Make sure that you have all the ingredients, utensils, and time required for preparing the dessert you have chosen.

ASPARTAME is a sweetener made by synthesizing two amino acids. Equal and NutraSweet are made with aspartame, which reduces carbohydrates and calories when used in place of sugar. **Caution:** During prolonged cooking and baking, Aspartame can lose sweetness and even become very bitter. It's good for use in cold products and can be added to hot and cooked foods after heating. For example, use it to sweeten hot drinks. It's also good for sweetening puddings, toppings, and sauces while hot, just after cooking. Just stir in, mix until dissolved.

BAKING EQUIPMENT is very important, so it's worth the extra cost to buy high-quality products. Heavy baking pans work the best because they distribute the heat evenly. Heavy aluminum pans are best for cakes. Non-stick baking pans work well and are easier to clean, but you have to use special utensils to avoid scratching them. As a rule, I avoid dark pans because they absorb heat more readily and tend to cause foods to crisp and burn. If you already have dark pans, you will have to learn to adjust the oven temperature. Ovenproof Pyrex, stoneware, and glazed earthenware are desirable for baking. Purchase an assortment of sizes, and stack them inside each other to save space. Make sure you have a Bundt pan, loaf pan, cheesecake pan, and large baking sheet. A large cake plate with a pedestal and a high dome lid is a must for showing off your cakes and pies. It has plenty of other uses too: Stack muffins and scones on it, or pile up the cookies. (Keep some tins for storing extras—if they last that long!)

BUTTER gives some recipes a better taste and texture. However, if you're concerned about fat content and calories, you may want to use soft tub margarine, which is lower in fat than butter or stick margarine. Fat-free tub spreads don't do much for the taste or texture of baked goods, so it's best to avoid them. For recipes that call for butter at room temperature or for creaming, set it out early. For recipes that call for melted butter, the microwave is the easiest method to use. Have unsalted butter or margarine available for baking when the recipe calls for it. When it's salted, leave salt out of the recipe. (I never use the "optional" salt.)

BUY and use fresh fruit when it is in season and priced reasonably. Your desserts will always taste better. Suggestions for freezing fruit are listed below.

CANNED fruit can usually be substituted for fresh, but be sure to use only fruit that has no sugar added. Drain thoroughly when using for pies or cakes. Canned fruit with its juice is good mixed into gelatin desserts. Mix drained fruit with no sugar added jelly for a topping or filling.

CINNAMON SUGAR can be made by mixing ground cinnamon with a sugar substitute such as Sweet 'n Low, Sugar Twin, DiabetiSweet, Nutra-Sweet, Equal, or granulated fructose. Use the amount of cinnamon that suits your taste. You can substitute cinnamon sugar for brown sugar in some recipes. Sprinkle it onto fruit or puddings. Prepare a larger quantity and keep it in a tightly sealed jar. Do not use the mixture made with Equal or NutraSweet if you are going to boil or bake with it. I prefer to make it with DiabetiSweet or Sweet 'n Low.

CREAM CHEESE is frequently used in desserts. I use the low-fat variety in many of my recipes. Also, I think the fat-free kind is just as good as the regular when it is mixed with cottage cheese or with low-fat ricotta cheese for cheesecakes.

DECISIONS are important! Decide which filling, topping, or sauce you might want to use with your dessert, and make sure the ingredients you will need are on hand.

EGGS (AND EGG SUBSTITUTES) are important ingredients. Because of the higher cholesterol in eggs, you may want to use a substitute. Remember that you can't use a substitute if the recipe calls for separated eggs. (But if you need whites only, you can now buy them alongside the egg substitutes.) Eggs are easier to separate while cold. Egg whites can be frozen and saved for later use.

FLOUR used in these recipes can be all-purpose, white cake, wheat cake, self-rising, or wheat. After flour is opened, it should be kept in tightly sealed containers.

FREEZE some items for later use: Cook fresh fruit compotes. Make applesauce. Cook black seedless grapes. The grapes, once cooked, will taste like dark red cherries. Cook with very little water because all fruits will make their own juice. Add sugar substitute or granulated fructose to taste. Some raw fruits can be frozen too. Peel and slice apples and add a little orange juice. Remove stems from seedless whole red, green, or black grapes. Freeze in plastic bags. A small dish of frozen grapes can be tasty and refreshing. They make great snacks for children. Most melons, peeled and cut in chunks or balls, can then be frozen. Freeze dark, sweet Bing cherries just as you buy them with the stem on. When you remove them from the freezer, let them sit for a few minutes before eating. Remember, the pit is still in the cherry! Blueberries, strawberries, pineapple, banana, and peeled chunks of mango freeze well. Use the blueberries in pies, muffins, and toppings.

GRANULATED FRUCTOSE is a natural fruit sugar. It is sweeter than granulated sugar (sucrose) and can be used for baking and cooking. It is not affected by heat or cold and has more substance than other substitutes. It works well when a recipe calls for creaming butter, margarine, or cream cheese together with a sugar substitute. It tends to make baked products more dense, so in some recipes, I suggest mixing another sugar substitute with the fructose. This combination reduces carbohydrates and calories in a recipe. I use granulated fructose quite often in my recipes. You will probably have to purchase it in a health food store where it is sold in bulk.

GREASE cooking pans with butter, margarine, or a cooking spray. When coating the bottom of a pan for a cheesecake, I use butter. The spray I prefer is Pam.

HEAT varies from oven to oven. Use your knowledge of your own oven to decide whether you should adjust the setting higher or lower. Because your oven may bake faster or slower, always keep an eye on what you're baking and test for doneness. When ovens are turned off, they stay hot for awhile, so unless otherwise indicated, remove your baked goods as soon as they're done. There are some exceptions, such as cheesecakes that are left in the oven to cool with the door open.

HEALTH FOOD STORES are where you may have to shop in order to find certain "sugar free" products or substitutes. Thank goodness that there are more of them around these days, perhaps because people are becoming more health conscious.

IMPROVISE where necessary. Sometimes it's necessary to change, add, substitute, or leave out an ingredient. Getting into the habit of tasting your recipe will help you decide whether you want to do any of these things in order to suit your taste. For instance, you may want to add a little more sugar substitute or granulated fructose. Perhaps you'd like some more cinnamon. At first you will probably make the recipe as written. If it's perfect for you, then you won't have to improvise. A simple way to change a recipe is to substitute the main ingredient but keep the same measurements. For example, use peaches, pears, or plums instead of nectarines (or vice versa) in a pie or cobbler. Try cooked, mashed yams or butternut squash in place of pumpkin.

JAMS AND JELLIES without added sugar make tasty additions to a great many of the recipes in this book. There are so many fruit varieties to choose from; whichever you choose, use a seedless version. Heating the jam or jelly will give it a nice shiny glaze when you spread it on top of a cheesecake. Before baking muffins, try adding a spoonful of jam or jelly to the center of the batter as you fill the muffin cups. Dot a little bit of your favorite flavor on top of cookies before baking. Use it when baking custard or swirl some in your puddings.

THE KNIFE TEST is one of the most important tests to do when baking. I prefer to use a dinner knife instead of a toothpick, but the choice is yours. When a baked dessert is done, a knife inserted into the center will come out clean. Custards and cheesecakes are tested the same way and will continue to set as they cool. Some recipes say "do not overbake," and in these cases the test will come out slightly moist.

LACTOSE can be difficult for some people to digest. I've tested my recipes with soy and rice milk in place of cow's milk, and the results have been good. So if you're lactose-intolerant, you may want to try these alternatives.

A LIGHT TOUCH is what you need when making pastry. Carefully follow the directions in Chapter 1, and you will succeed.

MAKE A LIST of the ingredients that are most often called for in the recipes of your choice. When it's time to shop, you can easily refer to the list and check the items that need replacement. Make several photocopies of your list so that you won't have to rewrite it. Another organizing trick is to put stick-on tabs in your cookbooks to mark your favorite recipes. Just write the recipe name on the marker for quick reference.

MARGARINE can be a good substitute for butter, depending on the taste and texture you are seeking. Health authorities aren't in agreement about which is better from a health perspective, so choose according to your preference and remember that moderation is the key. There are so many different brands to choose from. For unsalted margarine, I use Fleishmans, and my choice for regular margarine is I Can't Believe It's Not Butter. If you buy margarine in stick form, it will be easier to measure. However, soft margarine is lower in fat than butter or stick margarine, which are both 100% fat.

NEVER stop making desserts. Serve small portions. **Never** overeat. **Never** use granulated sugar (sucrose) if you have diabetes, and don't be tempted to try a dessert made with sugar, because a little leads to a little more and it becomes a habit and then you're in trouble! As you probably know, habits are very difficult to break!

OPTIONAL ingredients are included in the Nutrition Facts and Exchanges. You can decide whether or not to add these, based on your preferences. For example, I don't add the optional salt, but you may prefer to do so.

PERSIMMON is a wonderful, sweet fruit that ripens in the fall. However, if it's not fully ripe when you use it, it will be very bitter. If the persimmons at the store aren't fully ripe, select the ripest you can find, place them on a windowsill in the sun, turn them once in a while, and let them get fully ripe. (Place a piece of aluminum foil under them so that your sill doesn't get sticky. When ripe, cut the leaf off the top, remove the yellow stringy part (which is very bitter), scoop out the pulp with a spoon, scrape the pulp off the skin, and discard the skin. Measure the amount of pulp you need for your recipe and, if you're not planning to use it right away, freeze it in plastic bags or containers. Persimmon recipes are especially nice at holiday time.

READ the whole book of recipes from front cover to back. Most people never do this and they miss so much information that can be used to their advantage. They hunt, pick, and miss. Because you're reading this, you will be ahead of the rest.

SACCHARIN is a sweetener that has been used in foods for many years. Sweet 'n Low and Sugar Twin are saccharin based. Of the two, Sugar Twin is lighter and airier. The manufacturers suggest that you use the same measurements of Sugar Twin as sugar in a recipe, but I use a great deal less because it's much sweeter than sugar. The sugar substitutes used most often in my recipes are Sugar Twin and Sweet 'n Low. The way to decide which sweetener you prefer is to try all of them. They all reduce carbohydrates and calories in a diet.

TASTE your recipe as you put it together. A pastry chef always tests for taste. You can get a very good idea of how the finished product will taste by doing this. When you were a kid, did you clean out the bowl before it was washed? My husband still does it! That's sample tasting. I sample the dry ingredients in order to see if there is enough sugar substitute or granulated fructose. If it needs more, it's easier to mix in and distribute evenly when dry. Taste again after the wet ingredients are mixed in.

TEXTURE will never be exactly the same as baked desserts prepared with granulated sugar. Cakes and muffins will be smaller and more dense, but they *will* taste good. Some recipes will be less dense than others. I've tested and adjusted each of these recipes for the best taste and texture.

UNDERSTAND the fact that there are approximately 800 calories and 200 grams of carbohydrates in one cup of granulated sugar (sucrose). By using a sugar substitute other than fructose, you can eliminate most of the carbohydrates and calories. The American Diabetes Association now says that people with diabetes can use some sucrose. However, testing and monitoring prove that the use of sucrose by people with diabetes causes blood glucose levels to rise and fall rapidly. Granulated fructose and other sugar substitutes will raise the blood sugar level slightly but will not cause sudden surges; thus they are safe for consumption. Most people with diabetes experience a difficult period adjusting to a "no sugar" diet, because sugar can be habit forming. Now that you're off the sugar kick, it's best not to start using it again. Who needs the extra carbohydrates and calories? You will have to exercise longer and harder to burn them off. Remember to adhere to your diet, and always consult your doctor and dietician before making any drastic changes.

VERY PLEASED is how we should all feel now that we are able to enjoy delicious desserts designed just for us.

WHISK your dry ingredients thoroughly before you sift. Follow directions in the recipes for sifting. You can also use a whisk for beating eggs or egg whites and for mixing wet ingredients together.

XEROX your list of frequently used ingredients to make shopping easier.

YOU will be the judge! You may be thinking now that these recipes probably won't taste very good. After all, you've no doubt tried sugar-free dessert products from bakeries and grocery stores. Did you really love them? Did you finish eating them all or did you throw them away? Would you go back and buy some more? Of course, certain ones are okay, but the majority of them are not too appealing to the taste buds. Now you're wondering whether you really want to bother baking all these recipes. Do you miss eating tasty desserts? If so, try as many recipes as you can. Please let me know if you and your family enjoy them. If you don't like the recipes, I'd like to hear from you as well. I'll look forward to reading your ideas and comments. Mail to Without the Sugar, Jean C. Wade, P.O. Box 3611, Santa

Barbara, CA 93130 or P.O. Box 415, Pismo Beach, CA 99448, or Jean C. Wade, c/o Celestial Arts/Ten Speed Press, P.O. Box 7123, Berkeley, CA. 94707, Re: How Sweet It Is...Without the Sugar. If you like the book, please tell your friends and relatives about it. You might even want to bake some samples to give away—you may find that someone else that you know wants to bake without the sugar also. Check my web page for new information (www.withoutthesugar.com). E-mail (withoutthesugar@yahoo.com)

ZEST is flavorful and piquant, whether it's from oranges, lemons, or limes. To store zest for convenient use, whenever you're using one of these fruits, simply remove thin strips of rind (skin), place them in a plastic bag, and freeze. (Be careful not to include the white pith, which is bitter.) When you need some zest for a recipe, snip some frozen strips into bits with sharp scissors. This way you'll have the zest available whenever you need it. If you're zesting your fruit just before using it, grating is another good method to use. Zest makes a wonderful addition to almost all of my recipes, especially muffins, cakes, and puddings. Experiment a little—you will be pleasantly surprised and pleased with the unique, fresh flavor it will add to your desserts.

Equivalent Measurements

Ounces	Cups	Tablespoons	Teaspoons
1/2 oz.		1 T.	3 tsp.
1 oz.		2 T.	6 tsp.
2 oz.	1/4 c.	4 T	12 tsp.
4 oz.	1/2 c.	8 T.	24 tsp.
8 oz.	1 c.	16 T.	48 tsp.

Baking Pan Sizes

size	holds	size	holds
8 in. pie	2 c.	9 in. pie	1 qt.
10 in. pie	1 1/4 qt.		
8 in. round	1 qt.	9 in. round	1 1/2 qt.
8 in. square	2 qt.	9 in. square	2 1/2 qt.
9 x 5 x 2 in. loaf	2 qt.		
9 in. tube	3 qt.	10 in. tube	3 qt.
10 in. bundt	3 qt.		
9 x 5 in.	1 1/2 qt.	10 x 6 in.	3 1/2 qt.
11 x 7 in.	3 1/2 qt.		
3 x 9 x 2 in.	3 1/2 qt.	14 x 10 in.	cookie tin
15 1/2 x 10 1/2 x 1 in.	jelly roll		

Equivalent Sugar Substitute Measurements

DIABETISWEET

Granulated Sugar	Sugar Substitute
1/4 cup	3 packets or 1 teaspoon
1/3 cup	4 packets or 1 1/4 teaspoon
1/2 cup	6 packets or 1 tablespoon
1 cup	12 packets or 2 tablespoons

SUGAR TWIN

Granulated Sugar	Sugar Substitute
1 teaspoon	1/2 packet or 1 teaspoon Sugar Twin Spoonable*
1 teaspoon	1/2 packet or 1 teaspoon Sugar Twin Brown*
1/4 cup	6 packets or 1/4 cup Sugar Twin Spoonable or Brown*
1/3 cup	8 packets or 1/3 cup Sugar Twin Spoonable or Brown*
1/2 cup	12 packets or 1/2 cup Sugar Twin Spoonable or Brown*

*When baking, it may be necessary to experiment with reduced amounts of Sugar Twin to achieve the best results. Recipes calling for more than 1/2 cup of sugar are not recommended. I tend to use much less Sugar Twin than the equivalency. It's important to do the taste test as you mix the recipes.

EQUAL

Granulated Sugar	Equal Packets	Equal Measure	Equal Spoonful
2 teaspoons	1 packet	About 1/4 teaspoon	2 teaspoons
1 tablespoon	1 1/2 packets	1/2 teaspoon	1 tablespoon
1/4 cup	6 packets	1 3/4 teaspoons	1/4 cup
1/3 cup	8 packets	2 1/2 teaspoons	1/3 cup
1/2 cup	12 packets	3 1/2 teaspoons	1/2 cup
3/4 cup	18 packets	5 1/2 teaspoons	3/4 cup
1 cup	24 packets	7 1/4 teaspoons	1 cup
1 pound	57 packets	5 tbsp.+ 2 tsp.	2 1/4 cups

GRANULATED FRUCTOSE

The measurements below are based on using 1/3 less granulated fructose than granulated sugar. Fructose is not a reduced calorie food. Also keep in mind that, because it doesn't cause blood sugar to rise rapidly, it cannot be used to counteract low blood sugar the way concentrated fruit juices and sugar can. (But this same quality makes it good for use in desserts.)

Granulated Sugar	Granulated Fructose
1 tablespoon	2 teaspoons
3 tablespoons	1/4 cup
1/2 cup	5 tablespoons
3/4 cup	1/2 cup
1 cup	2/3 cup
1 1/2 cups	1 cup
2 cups	1 1/3 cups
3 cups	2 cups

NUTRITION FACTS
Serving Size: 1 Teaspoon   Carbohydrates 4 g.   Sugars 4 g.

DIABETIC EXCHANGE INFORMATION
1 level teaspoon = free food exchange
4 level teaspoons = 1 fruit exchange

NOTE: You must always do a taste test when cooking or baking with sugar substitutes. Granulated fructose is sweeter than granulated sugar, so you should reduce the quantity as shown in the chart above. I use even less granulated fructose than the amounts listed in the above chart; my measurements are usually half or less than the granulated sugar called for in a regular recipe. You may find that you also prefer to use less.

I always use granulated fructose in recipes where ingredients have to be creamed together, because the sugar substitutes do not have enough bulk for creaming. Sometimes I will combine granulated fructose with a sugar substitute. By all means, use your favorite sugar substitute for baking—just remember not to use anything that contains a great deal of aspartame, because it becomes bitter at high temperatures.

Basic Pastries

Pies, tarts, and cream puffs are popular, enjoyable desserts. They are pretty easy to make and do not require a long list of ingredients. I usually start with making the pastry, but some of you may prefer to buy prepared pastry from the store. There are mixes for double crusts, and pastry sticks that are one per crust. Pillsbury folded pie crusts are great. Ready-made pastry in a pie tin is usually smaller than the recipe calls for, but sometimes the deep-dish one will work. Before using alternatives, *make sure to check that there is no sugar added*! I am well aware that it may seem difficult to make your own pie crusts or shells at first, but practice makes perfect. Of course, it takes patience too! Rolling out pastry can be very messy. I'm sure many of you have mom's favorite recipe for the perfect flaky pie crust. By all means, if you have it perfected and it does not contain sugar, please use it. Remember, it takes practice to make good pastry, so don't be disappointed with your first attempt. For all the "pros" out there, you already know what I mean!

Hints for Making Pastry

The secret of good pastry is not to handle it too much—handling makes it tough and hard. Be gentle and quick. If you sprinkle water over the mixture haphazardly while tossing and stirring, there will be wet spots in the pastry that will stick to the rolling pin. Try to moisten a section at a time, pushing the moist dough aside and then adding water to the driest portion, so that all the dough will be just moist enough to hold together. The chilling step makes pastry dough less sticky. It will be easier to roll out and the finished crust will be flakier. Using too much flour when you roll out dough will make the crust tough and heavy. Have a gentle hand and use short strokes. When using a floured surface and rolling pin, check the pin and the bottom surface of the pastry to make sure that it does not stick. You may have to add more flour, but do so very lightly. Remember, heavy flour and too much handling spoil the crust! Some people roll out dough between two twelve-inch squares of waxed paper; a trick you may want to try. If the edges of the dough start to crack, press them together or patch them before rolling out—otherwise they will get larger. For a shiny top crust, brush with milk or slightly beaten egg white before baking. Here's a good trick for baking open single-crust pies: Buy a disposable deep-dish aluminum pie plate, or use one that you already have on hand. Punch lots of holes in the bottom of it, then invert the plate over the top of the filling in your one-crust pie. Leave it on until the pie is almost baked. Remove it and finish baking. Using this method, the steam escapes, your filling cooks faster, and the crust and filling will not burn. The inverted pie plate rim should fit right over the edge of the crust.

And the most important advice: Enjoy your desserts made with pastry!

Flaky Pastry for Single-Crust Pie

1 cup sifted all-purpose flour
1/2 teaspoon salt
1/3 cup very cold shortening, unsalted margarine, or butter
2 to 2 1/2 tablespoons ice water

In a bowl, combine sifted flour and salt. Cut in shortening with a pastry blender or two knives until mixture resembles coarse cornmeal. Sprinkle in ice water, one tablespoon at a time, tossing lightly and stirring with a fork. Try to moisten mixture in sections, pushing moist dough aside to add water to the driest portion. The dough should be just moist enough to hold together when pressed gently with the fork. Dough should not be sticky.

Shape dough into a ball and carefully flatten into a half-inch-thick round. Smooth edges to prevent cracking when you roll. Wrap in waxed paper and chill in the refrigerator for twenty minutes. Lightly flour your surface and rolling pin. Using short, gentle strokes, roll the dough lightly from the center out in all directions to 1/8 inch thickness. Form a circle one inch larger than an inverted 8- or 9-inch pie plate.

Fold pastry in half. Ease loosely into the pan with fold in center. Do not stretch. Dough shrinks slightly as it bakes and will crack. Gently pat out air pockets. Fold edge of crust under, press up into rim of pan, and crimp as desired. Pie is ready for filling. If you are prebaking an empty shell, prick entire surface with tines of fork. Refrigerate for 1/2 hour. If you prefer to prebake the crust, place in preheated 350° oven for 15 to 25 minutes or until browned to your taste. Cool before filling.

Serves 8

NOTE: Practice makes perfect, so don't be disappointed with your first attempt. For a fast, easy preparation, buy a pie crust without sugar. But it probably won't taste as good as this homemade version!

NUTRITION FACTS: Serving size-1 Calories 130 Protein 1.7 g.
Carbohydrates 12 g. Total Fat 8.4 g. Sodium 123 mg.

EXCHANGES: Bread .75 Fat 1.5

Flaky Pastry for Double-Crust Pie

2 cups sifted all-purpose flour
3/4 cup very cold shortening, unsalted margarine, or butter
3/4 teaspoon salt (optional)
4 to 5 tablespoons ice water

In a bowl, combine sifted flour and salt. Cut in shortening with a pastry blender or two knives until mixture resembles coarse cornmeal. Sprinkle in ice water, one tablespoon at a time, tossing lightly and stirring with a fork. Try to moisten mixture in sections, pushing moist dough aside to add water to the driest portion. The dough should be just moist enough to hold together when pressed gently with the fork. Dough should not be sticky.

Shape dough into two balls and carefully flatten each into a half-inch-thick round. Smooth edges to prevent cracking when you roll. Wrap in waxed paper and chill in the refrigerator for twenty minutes. Lightly flour your surface and rolling pin, and roll dough out as desired.

This recipe makes enough crust for one 8- or 9-inch double-crust pie, two 8- or 9-inch pie shells, eight to ten 3 1/2-inch tart shells, one 9- or 10-inch pie with lattice top, or one 8-inch deep-dish pie with lattice top.

To ensure that the top crust of your double-crust pie is tight and does not ooze, cut the bottom crust a half-inch larger than normal and fold it up over the top crust. Press firmly together for a tight seal. You may have to dampen the edge of the bottom crust with cold water to make it stick. Crimp as desired and cut plenty of slashes in the top crust to allow steam to escape.

Serves 8

NUTRITION FACTS: **Serving size-1 Calories 260 Protein 3.3 g.
Carbohydrates 23.8 g. Total Fat 16.8 g. Sodium 245 mg.**

EXCHANGES: **Bread 1.5 Fat 4**

Basic Chou Pastry

1 cup water
1/2 cup butter
1 cup sifted all-purpose flour
1/8 teaspoon salt (optional)
4 eggs

Preheat oven to 450°. Combine water and butter in a heavy saucepan or nonstick pan. Over medium heat, cook until butter is melted and water comes to a boil. Add the flour and salt. Stir vigorously with a wooden spoon until mixture is smooth and pulls away from sides of pan, forming a ball. Turn off heat and transfer mixture to a large mixing bowl.

You may use an electric mixer to beat in the eggs. Add first egg and beat until well mixed. Add remaining eggs, one at a time, beating well after each one until smooth. Cover lightly and let cool.

Drop pastry by heaping tablespoons for desired size of puffs, or spoon pastry into an icing bag with a 1-inch plain piping tube attached and pipe into desired shapes 1 1/2 inches apart on a nonstick or lightly oiled baking sheet.

Place baking sheet in upper third of oven and bake for 8 minutes. Reduce temperature to 350°. Depending on size of puffs, bake for 20 to 40 minutes longer until dry and lightly browned. Make sure they are completely done or they will fall. To test, remove one, cut a slit in the side, cool for 2 minutes, then open it. Center should be soft but not sticky or doughy.

When done, remove puffs from baking sheet immediately, place on racks, cut a slit on one side of each, and cool thoroughly before filling.

Makes 24 puffs

NUTRITION FACTS: Serving Size-1 Calories 47 Protein 1.6 g. Fiber .19 g. Carbohydrates 3.75 g. Sugars (trace) Total Fat 1.5 g. Saturated Fat 1.46 g. Sodium (trace) Cholesterol 41 mg.

EXCHANGES: Bread .24 Lean Meat .15 Fat .47

Basic Dense Sponge Cake

1 cup cake flour
1 cup all-purpose flour
1 teaspoon baking powder
3/4 cup cornstarch
1/2 cup unsalted butter, softened
1/2 cup unsalted margarine, softened
6 tablespoons granulated fructose
4 large eggs or 1 cup egg substitute
1 teaspoon almond or vanilla extract
1/2 cup low-fat milk

Preheat oven 350°. Prepare the pans of your choice (see note below) by spraying with nonfat cooking spray.

In a medium bowl, sift flours, baking powder, and cornstarch together twice. Set aside.

In a large bowl, use an electric mixer at medium speed to cream butter and margarine. Mix for 2 minutes until very creamy and smooth, scraping the sides of the bowl as you mix. Add granulated fructose and beat for another 2 minutes until light and fluffy.

Beat in 2 heaping tablespoons of the flour mixture. Add 1 egg or 1/4 cup of egg substitute and beat until smooth. Add more flour and egg alternately, beating after each addition. The batter will be very thick. Before beating in the last addition of egg and flour, add the extract to 1/4 cup of the milk, mix well, and add to the batter. Beat until smooth. Add the rest of the milk and beat thoroughly.

Spoon batter evenly into the prepared baking pans. Bake for 40 to 60 minutes, depending on the size of the pans, or until a knife inserted in center comes out clean. Remove from oven and cool 5 minutes. Invert pans on wire racks. Slice to fill layers when thoroughly cooled.

Serves 10

NOTE: This cake is more compact and densely textured than other sponge cakes. It is ideal to use with fillings because it is less crumbly. You may want to use two 8-inch cake pans with removable bases, dividing the batter evenly between them. I also like to use a 6-inch springform pan, which I fill halfway. Then I use a large muffin tin for the rest of the batter. You might even want to use all the batter for sponge cake muffins. Any of these varieties can be sliced and layered with your choice of filling.

NUTRITION FACTS: Serving Size-1 Calories 321 Protein 3.3 g. Fiber .68 g. Carbohydrates 28 g. Sugars 1.34 g. Total Fat 20 g. Saturated Fat 8.3 g. Sodium 391 mg. Cholesterol 111 mg.

EXCHANGES: Bread 2 Lean Meat .36 Fat 4

Creamy Custard

1 cup extra light or whole milk
1 teaspoon vanilla extract
1/4 cup all-purpose flour
3 teaspoons sugar substitute or 5 tablespoons granulated fructose
3 egg yolks

Pour milk into a small saucepan. Cook over medium heat to scald, but do not boil. Remove from heat and stir in vanilla. Set aside.

In a bowl, whisk flour and sugar substitute together. Blend well. Add the egg yolks and beat thoroughly with an electric mixer.

Pour the milk slowly into the flour mixture, stirring constantly with a wooden spoon until well blended. Pour the blended mixture into the top of a double boiler. Cook over simmering water, stirring constantly for 5 to 10 minutes, or until custard is thick and smooth. Never let the custard boil. Cool to lukewarm or chill.

NOTE: You can use this custard for filling cream puffs and éclairs. Swirl chocolate sauce into it to add variety. It can be used as a layer between crust and fruits in a flan, where it prevents the fruit juice from seeping into the bottom crust, thus keeping it crisp.

NUTRITION FACTS: Whole Recipe Calories 402 Protein 19.4 g. Fiber .78 g. Carbohydrates 36.2 g. Sugars 14.2 g. Total Fat 18.3 g. Saturated Fat 6.4 g. Sodium 153 mg. Cholesterol 648 mg.

EXCHANGES: Bread 1.3 Lean meat 1.2 Milk 1.2 Fat 2.5

Basic Crepes

1 cup all-purpose flour
1 cup nonfat milk
1/2 cup egg substitute or 2 eggs
1 tablespoon unsalted margarine or butter, melted

In a bowl, beat together the flour, milk, egg substitute, and margarine. Let stand for 30 minutes.

Spray an 8-inch skillet or crepe pan (preferably nonstick) with nonfat cooking spray.

Use medium to high heat and watch the crepes carefully. Lower heat if necessary to avoid burning them.

Stir the batter and pour a scant amount (1/4 cup) into the pan, tilting to cover the bottom. Cook 1 to 2 minutes, turn, and cook another 30 seconds to 1 minute. You have to be quick with these, and they're best if very thin. Place crepe on a plate covered with a paper towel and place in a warm oven. Stir batter each time and repeat the process to make 10 crepes. Keep warm until ready to serve.

Makes 10 crepes

NUTRITION FACTS: Serving size-1 Calories 75 Protein 4 g. Fiber .34 g. Carbohydrates 10.8 Sugars 1.5 g. Total Fat 1.7 g. Saturated Fat .35 g. Sodium 35 mg. Cholesterol .56 mg.

EXCHANGES: Bread .50 Lean Meat .20 Milk .10 Fat .23

Crepe Fillings

Thinly spread your crepes with all-fruit (no sugar) jams or jellies. You can also sprinkle chopped nuts on top of the fruit spreads for added taste and crunchiness. You can spread crepes with whipped cream cheese and place some very small, thin slices of fresh fruit on top. You may want to use just fruit because of the excellent flavors. Carefully roll up the crepes and place seam down on a serving plate.

NOTE: Be aware that fillings are not included in the nutrition facts or exchanges.

REMEMBER: To prevent bitter-tasting desserts, never bake or boil Equal or NutraSweet.

ABOUT THE FACTS AND EXCHANGES: Ingredients marked as "optional" are included. When the ingredients list offers alternatives (i.e., sugar substitute or fructose), figures are based on the first item listed. Sugar grams are always included in the total carbohydrate counts, in addition to being shown separately.

Chapter 2

CAKES AND CAKE SQUARES

Applesauce-Spice Squares

1 cup all-purpose flour and 1/2 cup wheat flour or 1 1/3 cup flour
   and 1/3 cup oat bran
1 teaspoon baking soda
1 1/4 teaspoons ground cinnamon
1/4 teaspoon ground allspice
1/4 teaspoon ground nutmeg
1/4 teaspoon ground ginger
1/8 teaspoon salt (optional)
1/4 cup vegetable oil or melted butter
1/4 cup egg substitute or 1 large egg, beaten
1/2 cup Sugar Twin or 5 tablespoons granulated fructose
1 cup unsweetened applesauce
1 teaspoon vanilla extract

Preheat oven to 350°. Butter or oil an 8- or 9-inch square pan or an oven-proof baking dish.

In a large bowl, whisk together the flour, baking soda, cinnamon, allspice, nutmeg, ginger, and salt.

In a bowl, mix together oil, egg substitute, sugar substitute, applesauce, and vanilla. Beat well. Add these to the dry ingredients and mix well. The mixture should be thick and may be a little difficult to mix well.

Spoon into prepared pan and spread the mixture evenly. Bake for 35 to 40 minutes or until knife inserted in center comes out clean. Cool on rack and then cut into squares.

Serves 12

NOTE: If desired, add 1/4 cup golden raisins and 1/2 cup toasted walnut or pecan chunks. If using raisins, cut Sugar Twin to 1/4 cup or granulated fructose to 3 tablespoons. For snack-size squares, cut into 24 pieces. These changes are not included in Facts and Exchanges.

NUTRITION FACTS: Serving size-1 Calories 117 Protein 2.4 g. Fiber 1.4 g. Carbohydrates 15.2 g. Sugars 2.5 g. Total Fat 5.3 g. Saturated Fat .56 g. Sodium 105 mg. Cholesterol .1 mg.

EXCHANGES: Bread .63 Lean Meat .08 Fruit .18 Fat 1

Apple-Raisin Squares
with Walnuts

2 cups all-purpose flour

3 teaspoons baking powder

2 tablespoons Sugar Twin or granulated fructose

1 teaspoon apple pie spice or 1/2 teaspoon each ground cinnamon and nutmeg

1/3 cup egg substitute or 1 large egg, beaten

1 cup nonfat milk or rice milk

1 teaspoon vanilla extract

1/2 teaspoon almond extract

1 tablespoon thinly sliced and snipped or grated orange zest

1/3 cup soft tub margarine or butter, melted

2 large sweet apples (Yellow or Red Delicious, Fuji, or Gala), peeled, cored, and chopped into 1/4-inch pieces (about 2 cups)

32 golden raisins (please count them)

1/2 cup coarsely chopped walnuts

Preheat oven to 425°. Oil or spray a 9 x 9 x 2-inch ovenproof dish or baking pan.

In a large bowl, sift together flour and baking powder. Add sugar substitute and spice. Whisk together until thoroughly mixed.

In a large bowl, use a fork or whisk to beat together egg substitute, milk, vanilla, almond extract, orange zest, and margarine. Stir in apple pieces, raisins, and walnuts. Mix well. Pour all at once into the dry ingredients. Stir and mix until all flour is moistened. Mixture will be thick and chunky. Pour mixture into prepared pan and spread out evenly. Bake 35 minutes or until knife inserted in center comes out clean. Cool for 15 minutes. Cut into 16 squares. Squares will have tasty, moist centers. Serve warm or cool.

Serves16

NUTRITION FACTS: Serving size-1 Calories 133 Protein 3 g. Fiber 1 g. Carbohydrates 15.8 g. Sugars 3.43 g. Total Fat 6.6 g. Saturated Fat 1 g. Sodium 125 mg. Cholesterol 13.6 mg.

EXCHANGES: Fruit .18 Bread .71 Fat 1.20

Norwegian Lemon Cake Squares

2 cups cake flour
1/4 teaspoon salt (optional)
1 teaspoon baking powder
1/4 cup egg substitute or 1 egg, well beaten
1/2 cup fresh lemon juice
4 tablespoons thawed white grape juice concentrate
4 tablespoons granulated fructose or 3 teaspoons sugar substitute
1/2 cup olive or canola oil
Zest of 1 lemon, grated or thinly sliced and snipped
1 cup milk

Preheat oven to 350°. Butter or oil the bottom and sides of a 9 x 9 x 2-inch square pan or use a nonstick pan.

In a medium bowl, sift together flour, salt, and baking powder. Set aside.

In another bowl, beat together egg substitute, lemon juice, grape juice concentrate, fructose, oil, and zest. Add milk and beat well. Pour the wet ingredients into the dry and beat thoroughly.

Pour the batter into the prepared pan and bake 45 to 60 minutes or until knife inserted in the center comes out clean. Remove from oven, loosen edges, and let cool completely. Cut into 10 squares.

Serves 10

NOTE: This cake has a unique texture. It rises very little and has a luscious, creamy center. It keeps well. I like it best refrigerated and served cold.

NUTRITION FACTS: Serving size-1 Calories 217 Protein 3 g. Fiber .7 g. Carbohydrates 24 g. Sugars 14 g. Total Fat 12 g. Saturated Fat 2 g. Sodium 111 mg. Cholesterol 2 mg.

EXCHANGES: Bread .87 Fruit .19 Fat 2.29

Pear Squares

2 cups all-purpose flour
1 teaspoon baking powder
1 teaspoon baking soda
1/8 teaspoon ground nutmeg
1/8 teaspoon ground ginger
1/2 cup butter or margarine, melted
1/2 cup egg substitute or 2 large eggs, beaten
1/4 cup cream yogurt or buttermilk
1 teaspoon almond extract
2/3 cup granulated fructose or 5 teaspoons (16 packets) sugar
   substitute
1 cup peeled and diced Anjou pear (1 large ripe pear)

Preheat oven to 350°. Oil or butter a 9 x 9 x 2-inch square baking dish or pan.

In a large bowl, whisk together the flour, baking powder, baking soda, nutmeg, and ginger.

In another bowl, beat together butter, egg substitute, cream yogurt, almond extract, and fructose. Stir into the dry ingredients until just moistened. Taste for sweetness and make adjustments if necessary to suit your taste. Gently mix in the pears.

Spoon batter into prepared pan and spread evenly. Bake for 35 to 45 minutes or until knife inserted in center comes out clean. Remove from oven. Cool 20 minutes. Loosen edges. Cut into 36 pieces and serve warm, or invert onto a rack. Cut when fully cooled.

Makes 36 small squares

NOTE: If you like the delicate flavor of pears, you will really enjoy this treat!

NUTRITION FACTS: Serving size-1 Calories 144 Protein 2.7 g. Fiber .64 g. Carbohydrates 19 g. Sugars 1.6 g. Total Fat 6.3 g. Saturated Fat 3.8 g. Sodium 126 mg. Cholesterol 16.1 mg.

EXCHANGES Bread .7 Lean Meat .2 Fruit .1 Fat 1.2

Nutty Persimmon Squares

3 cups all-purpose flour
1 1/2 teaspoons ground cinnamon
1/2 teaspoon nutmeg
2 teaspoons baking powder
1 teaspoon baking soda
1/2 teaspoon salt (optional)
1 1/2 cups persimmon pulp (3 large, ripe persimmons)
3/4 cup egg substitute or 3 eggs, beaten
1/2 cup orange juice with pulp
1/3 cup olive oil or other vegetable oil
2 teaspoons vanilla extract
1/4 cup sugar substitute or 2/3 cup granulated fructose
1 cup raisins (preferably golden)
1 cup coarsely chopped walnuts
1 tablespoon sliced and snipped or grated orange zest

Preheat oven to 325°. Spray a 9 x 9 x 2-inch square pan or ovenproof dish with cooking spray or use a nonstick pan. (I prefer to use ovenproof glass baking dishes for shallow cakes or squares because I can lift them up and check to see how the bottom and sides are browning. This gives me a chance to adjust the oven temperature in order to prevent burning.)

In a large bowl, whisk together the flour, cinnamon, nutmeg, baking powder, baking soda, and salt.

Cut the leaf and stem off the top of the persimmons. (Remember, the fruit will be bitter if not very ripe.) Remove yellow stringy part. Scoop out and reserve the pulp. Scrape remaining pulp off skin and discard skin. Measure 1 1/2 cups of pulp and place in bowl. Beat in egg substitute, juice, oil, vanilla, and sugar substitute. Stir in raisins, nuts, and zest. Add the wet ingredients to the dry and mix until evenly distributed and moist.

Pour batter into the prepared dish and spread evenly. Bake for 45 to 60 minutes or until knife inserted in center comes out clean. If it browns too quickly, lightly cover with foil. Be careful not to let it burn or dry out. Remove from oven and cool before serving. Cut into 32 squares.

Makes 32 squares

NOTE: This recipe is one of my favorites. Each square is a small, tasty treat, and they're relatively low in calories, but you must still have good control and not eat too many. If you want fewer grams of sugar, use 1/2 cup of raisins instead of a full cup. The recipe can also be baked as a loaf cake. Bake in a loaf pan and slice thin when serving. It keeps for several days, and it tastes better each day. It also freezes well. Your family and friends will enjoy it during the holiday season, because it can be served as a sugar-free alternative to fruitcake.

NUTRITION FACTS: Serving size-1 Calories 123 Protein 2.5 g. Fiber 1 g. Carbohydrates 17 g. Sugars 7 g. Total Fat 5 g. Saturated Fat .50 Sodium 93 mg. Cholesterol .12 mg.

EXCHANGES: Bread .50 Lean Meat .10 Fruit .50 Fat .50

Carrot Cake Supreme

2 1/2 cups all-purpose flour
2 tablespoons cornstarch
2 teaspoons baking powder
3/4 teaspoon baking soda
2 teaspoons ground cinnamon
1/2 teaspoon ground allspice
3/4 cup egg substitute or 3 eggs, beaten
1 tablespoon vanilla extract
1/4 teaspoon rum extract (optional)
1/2 cup canned crushed pineapple in natural juice
1/4 cup applesauce (no sugar added)
1/4 cup canola or olive oil
1 teaspoon (3 packets) Sweet 'n Low
5 tablespoons granulated fructose or 1/2 cup fructose and no sugar
    substitute
2 cups finely grated sweet California carrots
1 tablespoon thinly sliced and snipped or grated orange zest
1/3 cup raisins (preferably golden)
1 cup coarsely chopped walnuts

Preheat oven to 350°. Oil or spray a 9 x 9 x 2-inch square baking dish or pan.

In a medium bowl, whisk together and then sift flour, cornstarch, baking powder, baking soda, cinnamon and allspice. Set aside.

In a large bowl, beat together egg substitute, vanilla, rum extract, pineapple, applesauce, oil, sugar substitute, and fructose (or 1/2 cup fructose and no sugar substitute). Sift dry ingredients again, this time sifting them into the wet ingredients, a little at a time, and either hand beat or beat with an electric mixer on medium speed for 3 minutes. Stir in carrots, zest, raisins, and walnuts. Mix thoroughly by hand.

Pour batter into the prepared pan and spread evenly. Bake for 1 hour or until a knife inserted in the center comes out almost clean. The center of the cake will be slightly moist. You can bake it a little longer if you wish, but do not let sides or top start to burn. Carrot cake should always be moist, not dry. Remove from oven and cool. Cut 48 squares. Lift out with a spatula and mound them on a large plate.

Makes 48 very small squares

NOTE: Always remember that if you eat several pieces, your Facts and Exchanges must be altered. Self-control is necessary here!

NUTRITION FACTS: Serving size-1 Calories 65 Protein 1.85 g. Fiber .59 g. Carbohydrates 8.4 g. Sugars 1.4 g. Total Fat 2.8 g. Saturated Fat .21 g. Sodium 29 mg. Cholesterol .04 mg.

EXCHANGES: Bread .3 Lean Meat .2 Fruit .1 Vegetables .1 Fat .5

Chocolate-Custard Cake

1 cup all-purpose flour
1 1/2 teaspoons baking powder
1 tablespoon cornstarch
1 cup egg substitute or 4 eggs
1/4 cup low-fat ricotta cheese
4 tablespoons granulated fructose or 3 1/2 teaspoons Sugar Twin
2 tablespoons water
Creamy Custard (page 25), to be prepared while cake is cooling
2 ounces (2 squares) unsweetened baking chocolate
1 teaspoon (3 packets) sugar substitute or 2 teaspoons granulated
    fructose
1 tablespoon heavy cream

Preheat oven to 325°. Butter a 9-inch cake pan.

In a bowl, mix flour, baking powder, and cornstarch. Whisk together and sift twice.

In a bowl, mix egg substitute, ricotta cheese, fructose, and water. Using an electric mixer, beat until frothy. Gradually add the liquid mixture into the dry ingredients while beating. Mix well.

Pour batter into the prepared pan. Bake for 35 minutes or until knife inserted in center comes out clean. Remove from oven and cool for 10 minutes. Loosen edges, invert, and cool on rack. This cake will be thin and dense.

While the cake is cooling, prepare Creamy Custard. Set aside.

After the cake has cooled, prepare the chocolate topping. Use a small cup to melt chocolate squares in the microwave for 1 minute on high. Stir in sugar substitute until dissolved. Add cream and mix in quickly. The chocolate will thicken. Use flat bottom of cake for the top. With a table knife, spread the chocolate evenly over the cake from side to side. Spread over cake just once—don't try to add more. Save leftover chocolate, refrigerating it until hard.

Spread slightly warm custard on top of chocolate, swirling it decoratively. Let custard topping completely cool. Coarsely chop chilled chocolate and sprinkle over custard. Cover, making sure that it does not touch the custard. Refrigerate and chill for several hours or overnight before serving. It's best served very cold.

Serves 12

NOTE: This is a special treat. Slices will be thin and firm, and the chocolate under the creamy custard will crunch like candy as you bite into it. You can also insert fresh blueberries, raspberries, sliced banana, or strawberries into the custard. Decorate the top with berries or sliced bananas. These alternative additions are not included in the Facts or Exchanges.

NUTRITION FACTS: Serving size-1 Calories 137 Protein 6.21 g. Fiber 1.1 g. Carbohydrates 15.9 g. Sugars 1.6 g. Total Fat 5.79 g. Saturated Fat 2.77 g. Sodium 118.6 mg. Cholesterol 57.5 mg.

EXCHANGES: Bread .6 Lean Meat .6 Milk .1 Fat .9

Chocolate-Orange Cake

2 cups all-purpose flour

2 teaspoons baking soda

1 teaspoon baking powder

1/2 cup unsweetened cocoa

1/4 cup cream yogurt or buttermilk

1 cup unsweetened applesauce or vegetable oil

1/2 cup egg substitute or 2 eggs

3/4 cup fresh orange juice

2 teaspoons (6 packets) sugar substitute

3 tablespoons granulated fructose or 6 tablespoons fructose and no
sugar substitute

1 tablespoon sliced and snipped or grated orange zest

1/4 cup very hot water

1/2 cup coarsely chopped walnuts

Preheat oven to 350°. Lightly butter a 12-cup Bundt pan or equivalent baking pan.

In a large bowl, whisk together the flour, baking soda, baking powder, and cocoa. Set aside.

In a medium bowl, beat together yogurt, applesauce, egg substitute, orange juice, sugar substitute, fructose (or 6 tablespoons fructose and no sugar substitute), zest, and hot water. Add wet ingredients to dry ingredients. Mix together until combined. Stir in walnuts.

Pour batter into prepared pan. Bake on rack in middle of oven for 50 minutes or until knife inserted in center comes out almost clean. Cake should be slightly moist. Do not overbake. Remove from oven and cool cake in pan for 7 minutes. Invert on wire rack to cool completely.

Yields 28 thin slices

NOTE: You may want to use Creamy Chocolate Frosting (page 111) on this cake. Check your Facts and Exchanges first. You can also try 2 tablespoons of Cool Whip fat-free whipped topping, which has only 15 calories, 3 g. carbohydrate, 1 g. sugar, and 5 mg. sodium. I prefer to eat most of my desserts plain. For dieters and diabetics, it's best to eliminate the extras, but for guests without restrictions, it's nice to have some toppings or ice cream available.

NUTRITION FACTS: Serving size-1 Calories 63 Protein 2.4 g. Fiber .98 g. Carbohydrates 10.3 g. Sugars 1.88 g. Total Fat 1.78 g. Saturated Fat .29 g. Sodium 117.2 mg. Cholesterol .32 mg.

EXCHANGES: Bread .4 Lean Meat .2 Fruit .1 Fat .3

Choice Cheesecake

1/4 cup butter, softened

1 teaspoon brown sugar substitute

1 cup crushed shredded wheat

1 cup (8 ounces) cream cheese (33% fat free, neufchatel, or regular),
   at room temperature

3 3/4 cups part-skim ricotta cheese

3 tablespoons sugar substitute

4 tablespoons granulated fructose or 10 tablespoons fructose and
   no sugar substitute

1 tablespoon cornstarch

1 1/2 cups egg substitute or 5 large eggs

2 teaspoons vanilla extract

1/3 cup heavy cream

Preheat oven to 350°. In a small bowl, mix together the butter and brown sugar substitute, and spread on the bottom and 2 inches up the sides of an 8- or 9-inch springform pan, preferably nonstick. Sprinkle with shredded wheat. Brown in oven, being careful not to burn. Reduce oven temperature to 325° so it will be preheated for the cheesecake.

In a large bowl, cut the softened cream cheese into pieces and add half of the ricotta cheese. With electric mixer, beat together until smooth. Add the rest of the ricotta and continue beating until smooth and creamy. Beat in the combination of sugar substitute and fructose (or 10 tablespoons fructose and no sugar substitute). Beat in cornstarch until creamy.

Add egg substitute 1/4 cup at a time (or add eggs one at a time) and beat thoroughly into the mixture after each addition. Scrape bowl while mixing. Add vanilla and cream. Beat until blended together smoothly. Test for sweetness; if the mixture isn't sweet enough, add a little more sugar substitute or fructose and beat in thoroughly.

Pour cheesecake mixture into the prepared, cooled crust and place springform pan into a larger pan containing an inch of water. (If you use this method, make sure that the springform pan does not leak.) Place the pan on the middle rack of the oven for 45 to 60 minutes or until knife inserted in center comes out clean.

When the cake is set, turn oven off, open the door, and cool cake in the oven for several hours. When cool, leave the cake in the pan, cover tightly with plastic wrap or aluminum foil, and refrigerate overnight. The next day, loosen edges with a plastic knife, release springform pan, and remove outer ring. You may leave the cake on the base of the pan, but when you cut, be careful not to scratch. Use a plastic cake cutter. You can also invert the cake onto a large plate, then invert again onto another plate so it is right side up.

NOTE: Cheesecake is rich and filling, so serve thin pieces. The Facts and Exchanges are based on the cake without toppings. If you add toppings, check the Nutrition Facts on the packages and make your adjustments accordingly, especially for calories, carbohydrates, and sugars.

Makes 15 to 20 slices

TOPPINGS FOR CHEESECAKE:

Melt 3 or 4 heaping tablespoons of the all-fruit, no-sugar, seedless jam or jelly of your choice. When it is liquefied and smooth, glaze the top of the cake and cover with your favorite coarsely chopped nuts. Try using peach, raspberry, apricot, or orange marmalade, which is my favorite. Chopped walnuts are my choice, but maybe you like hazelnuts, pecans, almonds, or Brazil nuts. Try toasting your nuts in a small nonstick pan for richer flavor and a crisp texture. In season, use a glaze of strawberry jam and top with fresh sliced strawberries, or try the same with blueberry jam and blueberries. If you wish, you may want to mix the berries with some sugar substitute or fructose before placing them on the glaze. The glaze prevents the juices from soaking into the cake.

NUTRITION FACTS: Serving size-1 Calories 197 Protein 11 g. Fiber .33 g. Carbohydrates 9.8 g. Sugars 4 g. Total Fat 12.5 g. Saturated Fat 7 g. Sodium 182 mg. Cholesterol 36 mg.

EXCHANGES: Lean Meat 1.5 Fat 1.7

Fruity Nut Cheesecake

2 cups low-fat cream cheese, at room temperature

3 or 4 tablespoons granulated fructose or 6 packets sugar substitute
   and 2 tablespoons granulated fructose

3/4 cup egg substitute or 3 large eggs

1/2 cup fresh orange juice

4 ripe bananas, mashed

1 cup very finely grated carrot (1 large carrot, almost puréed)

1/2 cup heavy cream

30 golden raisins

1/2 cup coarsely chopped walnuts

Preheat oven to 350°. Lightly butter or oil a 9 1/2-inch nonstick springform pan.

In a large bowl, cut the cheese into small chunks. Add fructose and beat with electric mixer until creamy. Add the egg substitute gradually or one egg at a time while beating.

In a bowl, mix orange juice, bananas, and carrot together. (Make sure you use ripe bananas, and try to use a sweet California carrot.) Add this slowly to the cream cheese mixture while beating. Now add the cream and beat well. Just before pouring into the pan, mix in the raisins and nuts.

Pour batter into prepared pan and spread it out evenly. Place cheesecake on the middle rack of the oven and bake for 45 to 60 minutes, or until knife inserted in center comes out clean. Let the cake cool thoroughly in the oven with the door open. After cooling, cover tightly. Refrigerate 4 hours or more.

Serves 20

NOTE: This cake has a sweet, fruity flavor. Serve very cold in thin slices. Offer whipped cream as a garnish. If you find the cake too sweet for your taste, try again with less sugar substitute.

NUTRITION FACTS: Serving size-1. Calories 141 Protein 4 g. Fiber .78 g. Carbohydrates 11 g. Sugars 8 g. Total Fat 9 g. Saturated Fat 4 g. Sodium 89 mg. Cholesterol .2 mg.

EXCHANGES: Lean Meat .38 Fruit .48 Milk .11 Fat 1.16

No-Bake Fruit Cheesecake

3/4 cup crushed shredded wheat
1 1/2 teaspoons sugar substitute or 2 tablespoons granulated fructose
2 tablespoons melted margarine or butter
1 1/2 cups low-fat cream cheese, at room temperature
1 cup part-skim ricotta cheese, at room temperature
4 tablespoons granulated fructose
2 eggs, separated
1 small box (0.35 ounces) fruit flavored sugar-free gelatin
1 tablespoon plain gelatin
2 tablespoons cold water
3/4 cup boiling water
1 cup ice cubes
1 packet sugar substitute or 1/2 teaspoon granulated fructose
1/2 cup chopped strawberries

Preheat oven to 350°. In a small bowl, mix the shredded wheat, sugar substitute, and margarine. Spread on bottom and sides of a 9-inch deep-dish pie pan or 8 1/2 x 8 1/2-inch square baking dish. Bake 5 to 10 minutes until browned. Cool thoroughly.

In a large bowl, cut cream cheese into chunks and add ricotta cheese. With electric mixer on medium speed, beat until smooth. Gradually add fructose and beat thoroughly. Add the egg yolks. (Set whites aside.) Beat until very smooth. Set aside.

In a medium bowl, mix the 2 gelatins together. Add cold water and mix.

Add the boiling water and stir until gelatin is completely dissolved. Add the ice cubes. Stir constantly until mixture begins to gel. Remove and discard unmelted ice cubes. Beat with mixer until frothy. Add to cream cheese mixture and continue beating until smooth and fluffy. In a very clean small bowl, beat egg whites until stiff peaks form. Fold into cheesecake mixture very carefully.

Spread half of the mixture onto the cooled crust. Mix sugar substitute and strawberries. Stir strawberries into the remaining cheesecake mixture in bowl. Spread on top of the first layer. Refrigerate 2 hours or more. Just before serving, you may want to garnish each piece with a strawberry.

Makes 16 servings

NOTE: No-bake cheesecake can be made with many combinations of sugar-free fruit flavored gelatin and chopped fruits. Use fresh fruits when possible. Do a taste test when adding sugar substitute or fructose to sweeten, because some fruits need less than others. Blueberries can be slightly mashed or left whole. If using whole, add a few more than the half-cup measurement in the recipe. You can improvise and use well-drained canned fruit also. Enjoy this cold, refreshing low-calorie dessert on hot summer days!

NUTRITION FACTS: Serving size-1 Calories 89 Protein 7 g. Fiber .35 g. Carbohydrates 7.6 g. Sugars 2.6 g. Total Fat 3.3 g. Saturated Fat 1 g. Sodium 173 mg. Cholesterol 31.2 mg.

EXCHANGES: Bread .09 Lean meat .45 Fat .22

Peanut Butter Chiffon Cheesecake

1 1/2 cups crushed shredded wheat

2 teaspoons brown sugar substitute (optional)

1/4 cup softened margarine or butter

1 cup (8 ounces) low-fat or regular cream cheese, at room temperature

2 (15 ounce) tubs part-skim ricotta cheese

1 tablespoon cornstarch

3 tablespoons sugar substitute

4 tablespoons granulated fructose or 1 cup fructose and no sugar substitute

1 1/4 cup egg substitute or 5 large eggs

2 teaspoons vanilla extract

4 tablespoons unsalted peanut butter (preferably freshly ground)

1 tablespoon freshly grated or thinly sliced and snipped orange zest

1/3 cup heavy cream

Preheat oven to 350°. Rub margarine or butter on the bottom and 2 inches up the sides of a 9- or 9 1/2-inch springform pan. In a small bowl, mix the shredded wheat, brown sugar substitute, and margarine together with your hands. Pour into pan and spread on sides and bottom. Brown in oven, watching to make sure it doesn't burn. Let cool before adding the filling. Reduce oven temperature to 325° so it will be preheated for the cheesecake.

In a large bowl, cut cream cheese into pieces. Add one tub of ricotta cheese. With electric mixer, beat until smooth, add second tub of ricotta, and beat until very creamy. Add cornstarch, sugar substitute, and fructose (or 1 cup fructose and no sugar substitute). Beat until very smooth. Add 1/4 cup of egg substitute or 1 egg at a time, beating the mixture until fluffy after each addition. Add peanut butter, vanilla, and orange zest. Beat until smooth. Now beat in the heavy cream. The secret is to beat for 3 to 5 minutes, until very light and fluffy. The result will be a creamy cheesecake.

Pour filling into the cooled crust. Place the pan in a larger one containing an inch of water and bake on the middle rack of the oven for 1 hour or until knife inserted in center comes out clean. When cake is set, turn off oven, open door, and let cake cool for several hours in the oven. When cool, cover cake in springform pan with plastic wrap, and refrigerate overnight.

Caution: Make sure that the springform pan does not leak before you place it in water while baking. My experience has been that if you purchase an inexpensive pan, it tends to be loose when you close the ring, which means water can seep into the cake and ruin it. You may want to bake it without using water, but it turns out better baked in the pan of water. A good solution is to buy a good nonstick springform pan with a guarantee.

The next day, loosen edges, release pan, and remove outer circle. If you leave cake on the pan base, cut with plastic utensil so as not to scratch; otherwise, invert twice so that the cake ends up face-up on the serving plate.

Yields 20 slices

NOTE: For this recipe, I prefer to use the combination of sugar substitute and fructose rather than fructose only.

TOPPING:

Melt 3 or 4 heaping tablespoons of all-fruit orange marmalade (no sugar added) in a nonstick pan. (You may prefer another flavor.) When liquefied, glaze top of cake. Cover with your choice of coarsely chopped unsalted walnuts or peanuts. Of course you may prefer to leave the cheesecake plain without any topping at all. Cheesecake is very rich and filling, so cut it in very thin pieces and it will go a long way. It is possible to get more than 20 servings out of this cake.

NUTRITION FACTS: Serving size-1 slice without topping. Calories 168 Protein 9 g. Fiber .59 g. Carbohydrates 9.8 g. Sugars 3.8 g. Total Fat 10 g. Saturated Fat 3.9 g. Sodium 168 mg. Cholesterol 18.3 g.

EXCHANGES: Bread .17 Lean Meat 1 Fat 1

Dutch Apple–Raisin Cake

2 cups all-purpose flour

1/2 teaspoon salt (optional)

3 teaspoons baking powder

3 tablespoons sugar substitute or 3/4 cup granulated fructose

1 teaspoon apple pie spice

1/4 cup egg substitute or 1 egg, beaten

2 tablespoons apple or white grape juice concentrate

1/4 cup margarine or butter, melted

1 cup nonfat milk

45 golden raisins

2 large apples (Fuji or Golden Delicious) peeled, cored, and thinly
  sliced

Dash of cinnamon for top

Preheat oven to 375°. Oil a 9 x 9 x 2-inch baking pan.

In a large bowl, whisk together the flour, salt, baking powder, sugar substitute, and apple pie spice.

In a medium bowl, beat together egg substitute, juice concentrate, and margarine. Add milk and thoroughly mix. Stir in raisins. Pour all at once into the dry ingredients. Stir quickly until flour is just moistened. Stir three or four more times, but not until smooth.

Pour batter into the prepared pan and spread it out evenly. Arrange apple slices close together in two rows by pressing the sharp edges down into the batter. Slices should stand up straight and be very close together. Dot between the rows with margarine or butter. Sprinkle apples lightly with a dash of cinnamon.

Bake for 40 minutes or until golden brown and knife test in center comes out clean.

Apples should be slightly soft, not overcooked or burned on top. Remove from oven and serve warm or cool.

Serves 10

NOTE: If desired, while the cake is hot out of the oven, spread a thin line of all-fruit, seedless, no-sugar-added jam between the rows of apples. A little bit goes a long way, and you don't want to detract from the apple flavor. You could also add chopped walnuts to this recipe. Additions make things taste even better, but do remember that the Facts and Exchanges below do not include any additions. Remember to eat small servings—self-control is the key to managing your diabetes.

NUTRITION FACTS: Serving size-1 Calories 199 Protein 4.5 g. Fiber 2 g. Carbohydrates 33 g. Sugars 12.7 g. Total Fat 5.7 g. Saturated Fat 1 g. Sodium 288 mg. Cholesterol .56 mg.

EXCHANGES: Bread 1 Fat .07

Plain Layer Cake

2 cups sifted cake flour
2 1/2 teaspoons baking powder
1/2 cup margarine, butter, or shortening
1/2 cup granulated fructose or Sugar Twin
2 egg yolks
1 teaspoon vanilla or almond extract
2/3 cup low-fat milk
2 egg whites

Preheat oven to 325°. Oil an 8-inch layer cake pan with butter-flavored Pam, butter, or margarine, or use a nonstick pan.

In a bowl, sift flour and baking powder together twice. Set aside.

In a large bowl, cream margarine with fructose until light and fluffy. Add beaten egg yolks and beat thoroughly. Set aside.

Add vanilla to milk. To the creamed mixture, add the dry ingredients alternately with the milk in small amounts, beating well after each addition. Scrape sides of bowl to incorporate all ingredients.

In a small bowl, beat egg whites until stiff peaks form. Fold into the mixture.

Pour mixture into prepared pan and bake for 25 to 40 minutes or until knife inserted in center comes out clean.

Remove from oven and cool for 10 minutes. Loosen edges, invert, and cool on rack.

When thoroughly cooled, carefully slice in half to make two layers. Use the filling and topping of your choice. See Chapter 5 for ideas.

Serves 8

NOTE: This recipe could yield as many as 16 thin slices. If you choose to serve it this way, divide the Facts and Exchanges in half. And remember, frosting must be figured separately.

NUTRITION FACTS: Serving size -1 Calories 257 Protein 4.3 g. Fiber .65 g. Carbohydrates 29.5 g. Sugars 1.65 g. Total Fat 13 g. Saturated Fat 2.5 g. Sodium 263 mg Cholesterol 54 mg.

EXCHANGES: Bread 1 Lean Meat .25 Fat .23

Fruit and Nut Bundt Cake with Rum

3 cups all-purpose flour
1/4 cup wheat flour
1 1/2 teaspoons nutmeg
2 teaspoons baking powder
2 teaspoons baking soda
3/4 cup egg substitute or 3 large eggs, beaten
1/3 cup olive or vegetable oil
1/2 cup orange juice with pulp
1 1/2 teaspoons rum extract or flavoring
1 tablespoon sliced and snipped or grated orange zest
3 tablespoons sugar substitute or 8 tablespoons granulated fructose
1 1/2 cups mashed ripe persimmon pulp
1/2 cup golden raisins
1 cup coarsely chopped Brazil nuts

Preheat oven to 350°. Oil a 9-inch bundt pan with unsalted margarine or cooking spray.

In a large bowl, sift the flours, nutmeg, baking powder, and baking soda together. Set aside. In another bowl, beat together egg substitute, oil, orange juice, rum extract, zest, and sugar substitute.

Use a separate small bowl or measuring cup to prepare the persimmons. If the fruit is not very soft and thoroughly ripe, it will be bitter. Using very ripe fruit, cut off the leaf, remove the yellow stringy part, and scoop or squeeze out the pulp. Scrape the remaining pulp off the skin and discard the skin. Mash and beat the pulp. Add to wet ingredients. Beat together and mix in raisins and nuts. Pour wet ingredients into the dry and mix until thoroughly moistened.

Spoon batter into prepared pan and spread it out evenly. Bake for 1 hour and 15 minutes or until knife inserted in center comes out clean. It may be a little moist, but do not be tempted to overbake. Remove from oven and cool for 10 minutes. Invert pan on cooling rack. Cool thoroughly before serving.

NOTE: This cake tastes better when it is a couple of days old. It freezes beautifully for up to two months.

Makes 24 slices

NUTRITION FACTS: Serving size-1 Calories 160 Protein 4 g. Fiber 1.4 g. Carbohydrates 21 g. Sugars 7 g. Total Fat 7 g. Saturated Fat .87 g. Sodium 113 mg. Cholesterol .15 mg.

EXCHANGES: Bread .73 Lean Meat .13 Fruit .45 Fat .67

Wonderful Pound Cake

1 1/2 cups unsalted margarine or butter, at room temperature
1 cup granulated fructose
3 packets sugar substitute or 2 tablespoons granulated fructose
1 2/3 cups egg substitute or 7 large eggs
4 cups cake flour
1 teaspoon salt (optional)
4 teaspoons baking powder
1 teaspoon almond extract
1 teaspoon vanilla extract
1 cup nonfat milk, at room temperature
1 tablespoon or more thinly sliced and snipped orange zest (you may like a little more)
1/2 cup coarsely chopped walnuts

Preheat oven to 325°. Spray a 9-inch bundt pan or an equivalent size pan with a nonfat cooking spray, coat with unsalted margarine, or use a non-stick pan.

In a large bowl, with an electric mixer set on low to medium, cream the margarine until fluffy. Mix the fructose and sugar substitute together. Gradually add it to the margarine and beat well, scraping the sides of the bowl. Add the egg substitute or eggs, 1/3 cup or 1 egg at a time, beating well after each addition.

In a bowl, sift flour, salt, and baking powder twice.

In a measuring cup, stir almond and vanilla extracts into the milk. Add half of the flour combination and half of the milk mixture alternately to the egg mixture, a little at a time, and beat at medium speed. Then alternate the rest and stir in by hand, only until thoroughly blended. For a finer cake texture, use an electric mixer.

Pour half the batter into the prepared pan. Sprinkle zest, spreading evenly over the batter. Do not mix into batter. Sprinkle the chopped walnuts on top of the zest. Pour the rest of the batter evenly into the pan and smooth the top. Bake on the middle rack of the oven for 1 hour and 10 minutes or until a knife inserted in center comes out clean. Remove from oven and cool for 10 minutes. Invert cake on wire rack and cool thoroughly.

Makes 24 thin slices

NOTE: I like to use a bundt pan because the cake looks prettier. This is a rich cake, so it can be served in very thin slices and still be satisfying. The pattern of nuts and orange zest makes a nice design in each slice. It's especially good with freshly brewed coffee.

NUTRITION FACTS: Serving size-1 Calories 191 Protein 4 g. Fiber 67 g. Carbohydrates 19 g. Sugars 1.5 g. Total Fat 11 g. Saturated Fat 1.5 g. Sodium 251 mg. Cholesterol .5 mg.

EXCHANGES: Bread .77 Meat .28 Fat .18

Yellow Layer Cake

4 cups sifted cake flour
2 teaspoons baking powder
1 cup unsalted butter or margarine, at room temperature
1 1/4 cups Sugar Twin or 1 1/2 cups granulated fructose
6 egg yolks
6 tablespoons low-fat ricotta cheese
5 tablespoons nonfat yogurt
1 1/4 cups nonfat milk
2 teaspoons vanilla extract

Preheat oven to 350°. Oil two 8 1/2 x 1 1/2-inch round cake pans.

In a large bowl, sift together flour and baking powder. Set aside.

In another large bowl, cut butter or margarine into small pieces and cream thoroughly. Using electric mixer set at low to medium, gradually add Sugar Twin and beat until fluffy. Set aside.

In a bowl, use an electric mixer to beat together egg yolks, ricotta cheese, yogurt, milk, and vanilla.

Sift flour mixture into the creamed butter, a little at a time, alternating with milk mixture. Stir the batter by hand until well mixed. It will be quite thick.

Fill each prepared pan two-thirds full of batter and spread it out evenly. Bake 45 to 55 minutes or until a knife inserted in center comes out clean. Check carefully and test for doneness—if you overbake, the cakes will be too dry. Remove from oven. Cool 10 minutes. Loosen edges and invert cakes onto wire racks to cool thoroughly before decorating.

Yields 24 thin slices

NOTE: Choose the topping of your choice. Perhaps you'd like fruit and whipped cream or a glaze of all-fruit jam with chopped nuts. For this cake, I like to use Creamy Chocolate Frosting (page 111).

NUTRITION FACTS: Serving size-1 Calories 157 Protein 3.2 g. Fiber .27 g. Carbohydrates 14.8 Sugars 2.3 g. Total Fat 9.4 g. Saturated Fat 5.4 g. Sodium 63.8 mg. Cholesterol 75.4 mg.

EXCHANGES: Yellow Layer Cake Bread .7 Meat .2 Fat 1.8

Yum-Yum Coffee Cake

2 teaspoons boiling water
4 teaspoons instant coffee crystals
3 cups all-purpose flour
1 1/2 teaspoons baking powder
1 1/2 teaspoons baking soda
1 cup coarsely chopped walnuts
1/2 cup sugar substitute or 5 tablespoons granulated fructose
2 teaspoons ground cinnamon
1 teaspoon instant coffee crystals
1 teaspoon finely ground coffee
3/4 cup butter or low-salt tub margarine, at room temperature
1/2 cup (12 packets) sugar substitute
1 1/4 cups granulated fructose or 1 3/4 cups fructose and no sugar
   substitute
1/4 cup unsweetened applesauce
3/4 cup egg substitute or 3 eggs
2 teaspoons almond or vanilla extract
1/4 cup real sour cream or cream yogurt
1/2 cup low-fat ricotta cheese
1/4 cup cream yogurt or buttermilk

Preheat oven to 350°. Lightly butter a 12-cup bundt pan.
   In a cup, mix boiling water and instant coffee crystals until coffee dis-

solves. Set aside. In a medium bowl, whisk together flour, baking powder, and baking soda. Set aside.

In a small bowl, stir together walnuts, 1/2 cup sugar substitute, cinnamon, instant coffee crystals, and ground coffee. Set aside.

In a large bowl, use electric mixer set on low to medium speed to beat butter until smooth. Add sugar substitute and fructose (or fructose only). Beat until light and fluffy.

In a bowl, thoroughly beat together applesauce, egg substitute, almond extract, sour cream, ricotta cheese, cream yogurt, and reserved liquid coffee. Add these ingredients to the butter mixture and beat well. Gradually add small amounts of the flour mixture to the wet ingredients, beating well and scraping down bowl after each addition. Do a taste test. Add more sweetener if needed.

Pour half of the batter into the prepared pan. Evenly sprinkle the nut mixture on top of the batter and then add the remaining batter. Smooth out evenly.

Bake for 1 hour or until a knife inserted in several different places comes out clean.

Remove from oven and cool 10 minutes, invert pan and place cake on wire rack to cool.

Makes 28 slices

NOTE: Listen to the "yum yums" when you serve this cake—and be prepared to hear requests for seconds. Slice very thin pieces and you can probably have two slices without feeling guilty about cheating. With very thin slices, you will get more than 28 total.

NUTRITION FACTS: Serving size-1 Calories 165 Protein 3.9 g. Fiber .67 g. Carbohydrates 18 g. Sugars 1.4 g. Total Fat 8.66 g. Saturated Fat 3.8 g. Sodium 118.4 mg. Cholesterol 15.9 mg.

EXCHANGES: Bread .6 Lean Meat .4 Fat 1.6

Fantastic Chocolate Loaf Cake

3 tablespoons plus 1 1/2 teaspoons unsweetened cocoa

3 1/2 tablespoons boiling water

1 teaspoon sugar substitute or 3 teaspoons granulated fructose

3/4 cup egg substitute or 3 large eggs, beaten

1 1/2 teaspoons vanilla extract

1 1/4 cups sifted cake flour

1 teaspoon baking powder

1/4 teaspoon salt (optional)

1 tablespoon sugar substitute or 4 tablespoons granulated fructose

3 tablespoons granulated fructose or 7 tablespoons fructose and no substitute

13 tablespoons unsalted margarine or butter, softened and cut in pieces

Preheat oven to 350°. Oil a 4 x 8-inch loaf pan or use a nonstick pan.

In a bowl, stir cocoa and boiling water until smooth. Add 1 teaspoon of sugar substitute and mix. Add egg substitute and vanilla. Whisk together until smooth. Set aside.

In a large bowl, sift flour and baking powder together. Whisk in salt, 1 tablespoon sugar substitute, and 3 tablespoons fructose (or 7 tablespoons fructose only). Add margarine and half of the chocolate mixture to the dry ingredients. Beat with electric mixer set on medium until smooth. In two portions, add the rest of the chocolate mixture, beating well after each addition until very smooth.

Pour batter into the prepared pan and spread it out evenly. Bake in center of oven for 45 to 60 minutes or until knife inserted in center comes out clean. Cool pan on rack for 10 minutes. Loosen sides, remove cake, and place right side up to cool.

Makes 16 thin slices

NOTE: This is a small, dense, rich cake with a fudgelike center. You may want to cut the cake in half and fill it with plain whipped cream.

NUTRITION FACTS: SERVING-1 Calories 140 Protein 2 g. Fiber .55 g. Carbohydrates 9 g. Sugars .61 Total Fat 10.7 g. Saturated Fat 1.8 g. Sodium 186 mg. Cholesterol .23 mg.

EXCHANGES: Bread .37 Lean Meat .19 Fat .13

Lemon–Poppy Seed Tea Loaf

2 1/2 cups cake flour
2 teaspoons baking powder
1/2 teaspoon baking soda
1/2 teaspoon salt (optional)
1 egg beaten and 2 egg whites, lightly beaten or 3/4 cup egg substitute
2 cups applesauce (no sugar)
2 tablespoons vegetable oil
1 teaspoon vanilla extract
1/3 cup milk or lemon juice
1/4 cup granulated fructose or 3 teaspoons sugar substitute
1 1/2 tablespoons poppy seeds
1 tablespoon sliced and snipped or grated lemon zest

Preheat oven to 350°. Generously butter a 9 x 4-inch loaf pan.

In a large bowl, sift together flour, baking powder, baking soda, and salt.

In a medium bowl, beat together eggs, applesauce, oil, vanilla, milk, fructose, poppy seeds, and lemon zest. Gradually add to the dry ingredients, mixing until thoroughly moistened.

Spread batter evenly in prepared pan and bake for 55 to 80 minutes or until knife inserted in center comes out clean. Remove from oven and cool pan 10 to 15 minutes. Loosen sides, invert, and cool on rack right side up. Cool thoroughly.

Makes 18 slices

NOTE: This cake tastes great plain or with a little butter. You may want to offer sugar-free spreads or jellies as well. If you really like a lemon flavor, use lemon juice in place of milk. If not, use plain milk or a combination of milk and lemon juice. Try the loaf cake three different ways to see which you prefer, and always use the lemon zest.

NUTRITION FACTS: Serving size-1 Calories 95 Protein 2 g. Fiber .88 g. Carbohydrates 16 g. Sugars 3 g. Total Fat 16 g. Saturated Fat .41 g. Sodium 131 mg. Cholesterol 12 mg.

EXCHANGES: Bread .60 Fruit .22 Fat .39

REMEMBER: To prevent bitter-tasting desserts, never bake or boil Equal or NutraSweet.

ABOUT THE FACTS AND EXCHANGES: Ingredients marked as "optional" are included. When the ingredients list offers alternatives (i.e., sugar substitute or fructose), figures are based on the first item listed. Sugar grams are always included in the total carbohydrate counts, in addition to being shown separately.

CHAPTER 3

COOKIES, BROWNIES, AND BARS

Nutty Apple Brownies

1 1/4 cups all-purpose flour
1/4 cup unsweetened cocoa
1 1/2 teaspoons baking powder
1/4 teaspoon baking soda
1/2 teaspoon ground cinnamon
1/2 cup egg substitute or 2 eggs, beaten
1/2 cup tub margarine or butter, melted
1/2 cup sugar substitute or 5 tablespoons granulated fructose
2 teaspoons vanilla extract
1 cup peeled, grated apple
1/2 cup coarsely chopped walnuts or pecans (preferably toasted)

Preheat oven to 325°. Oil a 9-inch square ovenproof pan. In a large bowl, whisk together the flour, cocoa, baking powder, baking soda, and cinnamon very thoroughly.

In a small bowl, beat together egg substitute, margarine, sugar substitute, and vanilla. Pour the wet mixture into the dry ingredients. Mix thoroughly and then stir in grated apple and nuts.

Spoon the brownie batter into the prepared pan. Bake brownies for 25 to 30 minutes or until a knife or toothpick inserted in center comes out clean. Cool on rack, loosen edges, then remove from pan and cut into 1 1/2-inch squares.

Makes 28 squares

NUTRITION FACTS: Serving size-1 Calories 80 Protein 1.6 g. Fiber .60 g. Carbohydrates 6.5 g. Sugars .87 g. Total Fat 5.4 g. Saturated Fat .83 g. Sodium 77 mg. Cholesterol .09 mg.

EXCHANGES: Bread .27 Lean Meat .07 Fruit .04 Fat .08

Chocolate-Walnut Cake Brownies

8 tablespoons unsweetened cocoa

2 teaspoons sugar substitute or 2 tablespoons granulated fructose

1/2 cup boiling water

1 1/4 cups egg substitute or 5 large eggs, beaten

3 teaspoons vanilla extract

2 tablespoons sugar substitute

4 tablespoons granulated fructose or omit the 2 tablespoons sugar
   substitute and use only 9 tablespoons granulated fructose

2 1/2 cups sifted cake flour

2 teaspoons baking powder

1 cup softened unsalted butter, cut in pieces

1/2 cup softened margarine or butter

3/4 cup coarsely chopped walnuts

Preheat oven to 350°. Oil spray or butter an 8 x 12 x 2-inch ovenproof glass or ceramic dish or baking pan, or use a nonstick pan.

In a medium bowl, mix the cocoa, 2 teaspoons sugar substitute, and boiling water until smooth. When slightly cooled, add egg substitute, vanilla, 2 tablespoons sugar substitute, and 4 tablespoons fructose (or omit 2 tablespoons sugar substitute and use only 9 tablespoons granulated fructose). Mix thoroughly.

In a large bowl, sift flour and baking powder together. Add the butter, margarine, and half the cocoa mixture to the dry ingredients. Beat with electric mixer on slow to medium until mixed thoroughly. Gradually add the rest of the cocoa mixture while beating. Scrape sides of bowl and mix until batter is smooth. Stir in the walnuts by hand.

Spread the batter evenly in the prepared pan and bake for 35 to 60 minutes or until knife inserted in center comes out clean. Cool thoroughly and cut into 60 or more pieces. The "chocoholics" should like these!

Makes 60 pieces

NUTRITION FACTS: Serving size-1 Calories 79 Protein 1.3 g. Fiber .39 g. Carbohydrates 4.7 g. Sugars .29 g. Total Fat 6 g. Saturated Fat 2.4 g. Sodium 70.5 mg. Cholesterol 8 mg.

EXCHANGES: Bread .21 Fat .67

Chocolate-Chip Cookies

2 1/4 cups all-purpose flour
1 teaspoon baking powder
1 teaspoon baking soda
1/2 cup margarine or butter, at room temperature
1/2 cup granulated fructose or 5 1/2 teaspoons sugar substitute
1/2 teaspoon ground cinnamon
1/2 cup egg substitute or 2 large eggs, beaten
1 teaspoon vanilla extract
2/3 cup semisweet or bittersweet chocolate chips
2/3 cup coarsely chopped walnuts

Preheat oven to 375°. Set aside a large nonstick baking sheet.

In a bowl, whisk together flour, baking powder, and baking soda.

In a large bowl, cut in the margarine. In a cup, mix the fructose and cinnamon together. Gradually add to the margarine while creaming together thoroughly. In a cup, mix together egg substitute and vanilla. Add to the creamed mixture. Beat until smooth. Add flour mixture all at once. With a fork, mix it all together. It will seem quite dry. If it's too dry, sprinkle on 1 teaspoon of water and mix in. Add chocolate chips and walnuts. Mix and distribute evenly.

With a teaspoon or your fingers, form a cookie on the baking sheet and slightly spread out. Place on baking sheet fairly close together. They will not spread much while baking. Try to make sure that there are equal amounts of chips and nuts in each cookie.

Bake for 10 to 15 minutes or until lightly browned. Remove from oven, cool for 5 minutes, and place cookies on a rack to finish cooling.

Makes 44 cookies

NUTRITION FACTS: Serving size-1 Calories 74 Protein 1 g. Fiber .42 g. Carbohydrates 8.5 g. Sugars 1.6 g. Total Fat 4 g. Saturated Fat 1 g. Sodium 56 mg. Cholesterol 1 mg.

EXCHANGES: Bread .30 Lean Meat .05 Fruit .08 Fat .15

Drop Cookies

2 cups cake flour
1 teaspoon baking powder
1/4 teaspoon salt (optional)
1/3 cup softened unsalted butter or margarine
1/3 cup milk
1/4 cup egg substitute or 1 egg, beaten
1 teaspoon vanilla extract
2 1/2 tablespoons granulated fructose or 1 1/4 tablespoons sugar
   substitute

Preheat oven to 375°. Oil a large baking sheet or use a nonstick one.

In a large bowl, sift the cake flour, baking powder, and salt together twice.

In a bowl, beat together butter, milk, egg substitute, vanilla, and fructose. Combine the wet ingredients into the dry ingredients and mix thoroughly.

Drop cookies on the baking sheet by the teaspoonful, and bake in center of oven for 20 minutes, or until a toothpick inserted in center comes out clean.

Makes about 50 1 1/2-inch cookies

NUTRITION FACTS: Serving size-1 Calories 29 Protein .51 g. Fiber .10 g. Carbohydrates 4 g. Sugars .80 g. Total Fat 1 g. Saturated Fat .74 g. Sodium 32 mg. Cholesterol 3 mg.

EXCHANGES: Bread .15 Fat .23

Fruit Drop Cookies

2 cups cake flour
1 teaspoon baking powder
1/3 cup unsalted butter, at room temperature
1/3 cup white grape juice concentrate
1 teaspoon vanilla extract
1/4 cup egg substitute or 1 egg, beaten
1 cup chopped mixed dried fruit

Preheat oven to 375°. Oil a large baking sheet or use a nonstick one.

In a large bowl, sift flour and baking powder together twice.

In a medium bowl, beat together butter, grape juice concentrate, vanilla, and egg substitute. Gradually add the wet ingredients to the dry and mix thoroughly. Add the chopped fruit and mix in evenly.

Drop cookies by the teaspoonful onto the baking sheet and bake for 20 minutes in the middle of the oven, until toothpick inserted in center of cookie comes out clean. Remove cookies from sheet and cool on rack.

Makes 50 cookies

NOTE: You may use milk instead of white grape juice concentrate; however, the grape flavor makes these cookies taste fruitier. Using milk will change Facts and Exchanges.

NUTRITION FACTS: Serving size-1 Calories 38 Protein .54 g. Fiber .26 g.
Carbohydrates 6 g. Sugars 3 g. Total Fat 1.3 g. Saturated Fat .72 g.
Sodium 21 mg. Cholesterol 3 mg.

EXCHANGES: Bread .17 Fruit .18 Fat .23

Ginger-Lemon Cookies with Almonds

1 1/2 cups all-purpose flour
1/2 teaspoon ground ginger
1/2 teaspoon baking soda
1/2 cup finely ground almonds
1/2 cup unsalted butter or margarine, at room temperature
1 tablespoon (8 packets) sugar substitute
4 tablespoons granulated fructose or 8 tablespoons fructose and no
   sugar substitute
1/4 cup egg substitute or 1 large egg, beaten
1/2 teaspoon almond extract
1 tablespoon thinly sliced and snipped or grated lemon zest
2 tablespoons lemon juice

Preheat oven to 350°. Set aside a large nonstick baking sheet.
In a bowl, whisk together flour, ginger, baking soda, and finely ground
almonds. Set aside.

In a meduim bowl, using electric mixer on medium speed, beat together
butter, sugar substitute and 4 tablespoons fructose (or 8 tablespoons fructose and no sugar substitute) until fluffy. Scrape down the sides of bowl
while mixing. Add egg substitute, almond extract, lemon zest, and lemon
juice. Mix well. Gradually add dry ingredients and beat until smooth.

Drop cookies onto baking sheet by teaspoonfuls 2 inches apart. Dip fork
tines in water and press down on each cookie to flatten it out. For crisp

cookies, press them out thinner. Bake on middle shelf in oven for 12 to 15 minutes or until golden. Watch carefully so that they don't burn. When baked, remove from oven. Cool slightly. With a spatula, place cookies on a rack to finish cooling. When fully cooled, store in an airtight container with waxed paper between layers.

Makes 36

NUTRITION FACTS: Serving size-1 Calories 54 Protein 1 g. Fiber .29 g. Carbohydrates 5 g. Sugars .17 g. Total Fat 3.3 g. Saturated Fat 1.7 g. Sodium 21 mg. Cholesterol 6.9 mg.

EXCHANGES: Bread .2 Fat .6

Jelly-Almond Crescents

1 cup low-salt tub margarine or unsalted butter
2 cups all-purpose flour
1/4 cup egg substitute or 1 egg
1/3 cup plain cream yogurt, sour cream, or low-fat ricotta cheese
1 teaspoon almond extract
1/2 cup seedless all-fruit jelly or jam of your choice, no sugar added
1/4 cup ground almonds (not too finely ground)
1/4 teaspoon almond extract
1/4 cup unsweetened shredded coconut (optional)

Preheat oven to 350°. Oil a large baking sheet or use a nonstick one.

In a large bowl, using two knives or a pastry blender, cut butter into flour until it looks like small peas.

In a small bowl, beat together egg substitute, yogurt, and 1 teaspoon almond extract. Stir egg mixture into the flour and form a ball. Cover and chill for 3 hours to make dough easier to handle. (Sometimes, if the dough isn't too sticky, I'll roll it out right away.)

In a cup, mix together the jelly, almonds, and 1/4 teaspoon almond extract.

Divide dough into 4 pieces. On a lightly floured surface, roll each piece into a 10-inch circle and spread with the jelly mixture. Sprinkle some coconut on top. Cut each circle into 16 wedges. Starting at the wide end, carefully roll each wedge into a crescent.

Place crescents on the baking sheet 1/2 inch apart with point seam down. Bake 20 to 30 minutes, or until golden brown. Remove from oven. Cool 10 minutes, loosen crescents with a spatula, and place each on a wire rack to cool. You can eat these warm if you like.

Yields 64

NUTRITION FACTS: Serving size-1 Calories 49 Protein .69 g. Fiber .26 g. Carbohydrates 3.7 g. Sugars .87 g. Total Fat 3.4 g. Saturated Fat .6 g. Sodium 40.8 mg. Cholesterol .16 mg.

EXCHANGES: Bread .2 Fat .7

Nutty Spice Cookies

2 cups cake flour
2 teaspoons ground allspice
1/2 cup softened unsalted butter
1/2 cup softened margarine or butter
3 1/2 tablespoons granulated fructose
3 tablespoons sugar substitute or 3 tablespoons granulated fructose
1/2 cup egg substitute or 2 eggs
1 tablespoon thinly sliced and snipped or grated orange zest (optional)
1/2 cup chopped nuts (unsalted walnuts, almonds, Brazil nuts,
   hazelnuts, or peanuts)

Preheat oven to 375°. Lightly oil a baking sheet or use a nonstick one.

In a medium bowl, sift together flour and allspice. Set aside.

In a large bowl, cream butter, margarine, fructose, and sugar substitute (or 6 1/2 tablespoons fructose and no sugar substitute.) Add egg substitute and orange zest. Mix well with electric mixer. On low speed, add flour mixture gradually, mixing well and scraping bowl. Stir in nuts.

With a teaspoon, drop cookies onto the baking sheet 2 inches apart. Dip fork tines in water and flatten to make thin cookies.

Bake 15 to 20 minutes until cookies are lightly browned around edges. Check often and do not overbake. When baked, remove cookies and cool completely on a wire rack. Store them in an airtight tin.

Makes 40 cookies

NOTE: You can also prepare this recipe without nuts. Before baking, after you flatten the cookie, place some all-fruit, no-sugar-added jelly or jam in the center. Bake and enjoy! The jelly variation is not included in the Facts or Exchanges.

NUTRITION FACTS: Serving size-1 Calories 77 Protein 1 g. Fiber .33 g. Carbohydrates 5 g. Sugars .29 g. Total Fat 6 g. Saturated Fat 2 g. Sodium 68 mg. Cholesterol 6 mg.

EXCHANGES: Bread .22 Lean Meat .09 Fat .63

Old Time Oatmeal-Raisin Ice Box Cookies

1 cup butter, at room temperature
5 tablespoons granulated fructose
1 cup all-purpose flour
1/4 teaspoon ground nutmeg
1 teaspoon baking soda
2 teaspoons vanilla extract
2 cups rolled oats or 6-grain cereal (if you really want them crunchy)
40 golden raisins
1 cup coarsely chopped walnuts

In a large bowl, using an electric mixer set on slow to medium, cream butter and fructose until light and fluffy.

In a bowl, whisk together flour, nutmeg, and baking soda. Gradually beat this into the butter mixture. By hand, mix in vanilla and then the oats. Mix in the raisins and then the chopped nuts. The dough will be thick.

Divide dough in half. Roll out a sheet of waxed paper for each dough section. Fold waxed paper over dough and roll up into a log—the dough log will be covered with several layers of waxed paper. Repeat this with the second log. Logs should be about 10 inches long. Fold the ends under or tie them. Refrigerate for at least 6 hours.

Preheat oven to 350° when ready to bake. Remove waxed paper and cut dough into 1/2-inch-thick slices. Place each slice on an ungreased baking sheet. Using your fingers or a fork, push down on each cookie to spread it out a little. Cookies can be placed close together. Bake for 15 to 20 minutes or until medium brown. Be careful not to let the edges burn. (Don't be afraid to test one. Be gentle—they tend to fall apart when hot, especially if you use 6-grain cereal.) By testing, you can make sure the cookies don't end up over- or underbaked. When baked, remove from oven. Cool for 5 minutes. Use a spatula to place cookies on racks that are covered with paper towels. Cool thoroughly.

Makes 36 cookies

NOTE: Of course, in these modern days we call them refrigerator cookies, but don't you like the nostalgic phrase ice box? I would guess that many of you have never used an ice box. I needed these cookies in a hurry one day, so I baked them without chilling the dough first, and they turned out great. The cookie dough will keep for up to three weeks in the refrigerator. You can also prepare a double batch and freeze some for later. Bake fresh, hot cookies whenever you like. Kids love them after school, especially when friends come over to play.

NUTRITION FACTS: Serving size-1. Calories 112 Protein 1.6 g. Fiber .77 g. Carbohydrates 10 g. Sugars 2.7 g. Total Fat 7.5 g. Saturated Fat 3.4 g. Sodium 76 mg. Cholesterol 13.8 mg.

EXCHANGES: Bread .38 Fruit .17 Fat 1

Peanut Butter–Orange Cookies with Crisped Rice

3/4 cup unsalted margarine or butter, at room temperature
1/2 cup granulated fructose
1/2 teaspoon ground cinnamon
1 teaspoon vanilla extract
1/2 cup egg substitute or 2 eggs, beaten
12 heaping tablespoons chunky peanut butter
1 2/3 cups all-purpose flour
1/2 teaspoon baking powder
1 tablespoon thinly sliced and snipped or grated orange zest
4 tablespoons orange marmalade, no sugar added
2 cups unsweetened crisped rice cereal

Preheat oven to 375°. In a large bowl, cream margarine until light and fluffy. Mix together the fructose and cinnamon. Gradually add to margarine. Beat thoroughly. Mix vanilla with egg substitute and add to the creamed mixture. Add peanut butter and beat until thoroughly mixed.

In a measuring cup, mix together flour and baking powder. Pour into sifter. Sift half at a time into the peanut butter mixture. Blend thoroughly each time. Stir in zest and marmalade. Distribute evenly. Taste the mixture. Add more marmalade if needed.

Divide cookie mixture into three batches. Prepare each batch just before baking. Do not prepare ahead or the cereal will get soggy. Add about 2/3 cup cereal to each batch. Quickly stir in with a fork. Mix so that all cookies have some rice crispies. Drop a half-forkful of dough onto a large baking sheet, placing cookies one inch apart. When the sheet is full, dip fork tines in water and press down on each cookie. Bake 8 to 12 minutes on rack in middle of oven. When lightly browned, remove and cool a few minutes. Use a spatula to place cookies on racks covered with paper towels.

Makes 8 dozen (96) cookies

NUTRITION FACTS: Serving size-1 Calories 40 Protein 1 g. Fiber .23 g. Carbohydrates 4 g. Sugars .31 g. Total Fat 2.6 g. Saturated Fat .43 g. Sodium 38 mg. Cholesterol .03 mg.

EXCHANGES: Bread .12 Lean Meat .08 Fat .16

Shortbread Jam Cookies

1/2 cup unsalted butter or low salt tub margarine, at room temperature

2 1/2 or 3 tablespoons granulated fructose or 2 teaspoons sugar substitute

1/2 teaspoon almond or vanilla extract

1 1/2 cups all-purpose flour

2 tablespoons no-sugar-added, seedless raspberry or apricot jam

Preheat oven to 375°.

In a bowl, beat together butter, fructose, and almond extract until soft, pale, and fluffy. Gradually add flour in small amounts. Beat until smooth. When it becomes thick, knead with your hands until smooth. Knead in a slight bit more flour if it's too sticky, but it should be just right. Form a ball in the bowl.

From the dough ball, pull off pieces the size of a rounded teaspoon and place 1/2-inch apart on a large baking sheet. Form 32 dough mounds, each about the size of a rounded teaspoon. Do not flatten. After placing all the mounds, use your index finger to slightly indent each cookie and add a small dab of jelly.

Bake 15 to 25 minutes, watching carefully so that cookies do not burn. Edges should be lightly golden. Remove from oven. Cool 10 minutes. Tranfer cookies to paper towels on rack.

Makes 32 cookies

NOTE: This is one of my very favorite cookie recipes. I vigorously beat my ingredients by hand, but if you like, you can use an electric mixer set on low to medium. Try a variety of jams and jellies for different flavors. The 32 cookies in this recipe are sized for grown-up kids at heart. If you prefer, you can bake 64 small cookies for the little kids and cut the Facts and Exchanges in half.

NUTRITION FACTS: Serving size-1 Calories 25 Protein .29 g. Fiber .09 Carbohydrates 2.6 g. Sugars .22 g. Total Fat 1.5 g. Saturated Fat .9 g. Sodium .33 mg. Cholesterol 3.9 mg.

EXCHANGES: Bread .1 Fat .3

Tangy Norwegian Lemon Bars

1 3/4 cup all-purpose flour

1 1/4 teaspoons baking powder

4 packets sugar substitute or 3 tablespoons granulated fructose
   (optional)

1/2 cup melted margarine or butter

LEMON FILLING

7 tablespoons cornstarch

1 1/2 cups warm water

3 egg yolks, well beaten

2 tablespoons margarine or butter

12 packets sugar substitute or 1/2 cup granulated fructose

1 teaspoon thinly sliced and snipped or grated lemon zest

1/2 cup fresh lemon juice

1 lemon for slicing

Preheat oven to 350°. Set aside a 7 x 11 x 2-inch ovenproof glass or ceramic baking dish.

In a medium bowl, whisk together flour, baking powder, and sugar substitute. If you don't want a sweet crust, omit the sweetener. (I prefer it sweetened.) Add the melted margarine to the dry ingredients and mix together by hand. If a little more liquid is needed to form the dough into a ball, add just enough water to hold it together.

Using your fingers, pat and spread dough to cover bottom and sides of baking dish. Bake for 20 to 35 minutes, checking frequently for doneness. When it starts to brown and feels firmly baked to the touch, remove from oven. Cool completely before adding the filling.

For filling, place cornstarch in a 3-cup saucepan and add just enough cold water to mix together until smooth. Add warm water. Cook over medium heat, stirring constantly, until thick and clear. Remove from heat and cool slightly. Stir half of mixture into beaten egg yolks, mix, and add to the saucepan. Cook over low heat for 2 to 3 minutes, stirring constantly. Stir in margarine, remove from heat, and add sugar substitute, zest, and juice. Stir until smooth. While hot, taste for sweetness. It should be just right, but if you like, you can add a little more sweetener or lemon juice or both. Don't add too much, though—filling should not be thin. It should be like thick pudding.

Cool slightly and pour into baked shell. Before serving, slice 1 lemon very thin, remove seeds, and arrange halved lemon slices in rows on top of filling. Make sure you eat the lemon slice with the bar. This one is a real treat for lemon lovers!

Makes 16 servings.

NUTRITION FACTS: Serving-1 Calories 166 Protein 2.5 g. Fiber 38 g. Carbohydrates 20 g. Sugars 7 g. Total Fat 9 g. Saturated Fat 2 g. Sodium 97 mg. Cholesterol 39.5 mg.

EXCHANGES: Bread .69 Lean Meat .18 Fruit .50 Fat 1.39

REMEMBER: To prevent bitter-tasting desserts, never bake or boil Equal or NutraSweet.

ABOUT THE FACTS AND EXCHANGES: Ingredients marked as "optional" are included. When the ingredients list offers alternatives (i.e., sugar substitute or fructose), figures are based on the first item listed. Sugar grams are always included in the total carbohydrate counts, in addition to being shown separately.

CHAPTER 4

COBBLERS, CRISPS, AND PIES

Pear Clafouti

4 or 5 medium to large Anjou or Bartlett pears
Ground cinnamon
Ground ginger
2 tablespoons margarine or butter, melted
1/2 cup egg substitute or 2 eggs, beaten
1 teaspoon vanilla extract
2/3 cup half-and-half or whipping cream
5 tablespoons all-purpose flour
1/2 teaspoon baking powder
1 tablespoon sugar substitute or 2 1/2 tablespoons granulated fructose
1/4 teaspoon ground nutmeg

Preheat oven to 375°. Lightly oil or spray an ovenproof 9-inch glass or ceramic deep-dish pie plate. Peel pears, slice them, and arrange half the slices in the pie plate. Sprinkle with cinnamon and ginger. Place the rest of the slices on top.

In a small bowl, mix margarine, egg substitute, vanilla, and half-and-half. Beat together until creamy. Set aside.

In a bowl, whisk together flour, baking powder, sugar substitute, and nutmeg. Add the wet ingredients. Use electric mixer to beat until almost fluffy. Spoon evenly over the pears, making sure all the pears are coated. Bake for 45 to 60 minutes or until puffed and lightly browned.

Serves 8

NOTE: If you like pears, you will love this dessert. You can also make this with no-sugar-added canned pears. Simply drain, slice, and pat dry. Of course, fresh is the best. This dish can be served warm or cold. Offer sugar-free whipped cream for a topping if desired. Remember that extras are not accounted for in Facts and Exchanges. Enjoy!

NUTRITION FACTS: Serving size-1 Calories 145 Protein 3 g. Fiber 3 g. Carbohydrates 18 g. Sugars 11.5 g. Total Fat 7 g. Saturated Fat 2 g. Sodium 85 mg. Cholesterol 8 mg.

EXCHANGES: Bread .20 Lean Meat .25 Fruit 1 Fat .61

Seasonal Fruit Clafouti

3 or 4 ripe peaches, pears, or nectarines (or a combination)
1 teaspoon sugar substitute (brown or white) or granulated fructose
1/2 cup egg substitute or 2 eggs, beaten
2/3 cup regular or low-fat ricotta cheese
2 tablespoons margarine or butter, melted and cooled
1 teaspoon vanilla extract
2 tablespoons all-purpose flour
1/8 teaspoon salt (optional)
1 teaspoon ground cinnamon
1 teaspoon sugar substitute or 1 tablespoon granulated fructose
1/4 teaspoon ground nutmeg

Preheat oven to 375°. Lightly butter or oil an 8- or 9-inch ovenproof pie plate.

Peel the fruit. (Nectarines do not need to be peeled.) Slice and arrange the fruit in the pie plate, using a pinwheel design. If you are using a combination of fruits, alternate them. Lightly sprinkle 1 teaspoon of sugar substitute over the fruit.

In a medium bowl, beat together the egg substitute, ricotta cheese, margarine, and vanilla. In a small bowl, whisk together the flour, salt, cinnamon, and sugar substitute. Add to the wet ingredients. Beat until light and smooth. Test for sweetness, adding more sweetener if necessary. Spoon over the fruit, making sure all pieces are coated. Top with nutmeg.

Bake for 35 to 50 minutes until lightly browned. Insert knife to see if it comes out clean. When done, remove from oven and serve warm or cold.

Serves 8

NUTRITION FACTS: Serving size-1 Calories 101 Protein 4.5 g. Fiber .61 g. Carbohydrates 7 g. Sugars 4.7 g. Total Fat 6 g. Saturated Fat 2 g. Sodium 123 mg. Cholesterol 6.5 mg.

EXCHANGES: Lean Meat .58 Fruit .76 Fat .40

Nectarine Bottom-Crust Cobbler

6 medium or 4 large ripe nectarines (see below)
1 teaspoon sugar substitute or 3 tablespoons granulated fructose
1/4 cup water
1/2 cup margarine or butter
1 cup all-purpose flour
3 teaspoons granulated fructose
1 teaspoon baking powder
3/4 cup low-fat milk
2 tablespoons coarsely chopped walnuts
1 teaspoon cinnamon sugar (see below)

Preheat oven to 375°. Leaving skin on, slice nectarines and place into a saucepan. Sprinkle on sugar substitute and add water. Bring to a boil and cook until slightly soft but not mushy. Measure 2 cups of nectarines with very little juice.

Melt margarine or butter. Pour into a 9 x 9 x 2-inch ovenproof clear glass baking dish. (I use glass because it's easier to check the crust.)

In a bowl, whisk together flour, fructose, and baking powder. Add milk and mix together by hand. Spoon over melted butter by the tablespoonful. Sprinkle chopped walnuts over each spoonful of dough.

Spoon cooked nectarines over dough. Make cinnamon sugar by mixing ground cinnamon and granulated fructose or sugar substitute of your choice (other than aspartame). Mix to suit your taste. Sprinkle 1 teaspoon over nectarines.

Bake for 45 minutes or more. To test for doneness, remove from oven and lift a portion of the cobbler with a spatula or large spoon to see if the bottom is brown. The crust should be brown and crispy, but be careful not to burn it.

Serves 16

NOTE: This is so good served warm! Offer whipped cream for those who can't do without. You can bet that everyone will ask for seconds, so make sure you have enough when company comes. It disappears quickly! Bake a second one if need be. I make this recipe when I'm cooking a large quantity of nectarines for a compote. I can dish out the amount that is called for in the recipe and have more left for other desserts or for another cobbler. Never overcook the fruit. If you are cooking a larger quantity, adjust the amount of sugar substitute or granulated fructose to taste.

NUTRITION FACTS: Serving size-1 Calories 138. Protein 2 g. Fiber .78 g. Carbohydrates 13 g. Sugars 4.3 g. Total Fat 9 g. Saturated Fat 1.5 g. Sodium 125 mg. Cholesterol 1 mg.

EXCHANGES: Bread .43 Fruit .24 Milk .06 Fat .06

Peach Cobbler

4 cups very ripe peeled and sliced peaches

3 tablespoons sugar substitute or 5 tablespoons granulated fructose

1 tablespoon quick tapioca, uncooked

1 tablespoon fresh lemon or lime juice

1/2 teaspoon ground cinnamon

1/8 teaspoon ground nutmeg or ground cloves

1 cup all-purpose flour

1 tablespoon sugar substitute or 2 teaspoons granulated fructose

1 teaspoon baking powder

3 tablespoons cold margarine or butter, cut into small pieces

4 to 5 tablespoons skim milk or water

Preheat oven to 375°. In a large bowl, combine the peaches, sugar substitute, tapioca, juice, cinnamon, and nutmeg and toss well. Place in a 9-inch ceramic, glass, or nonstick pie plate. Set aside for 15 minutes.

In a bowl, whisk together flour, sugar substitute, and baking powder. Cut in margarine or butter with knives or a pastry blender. Stir in skim milk or water and form dough into a ball. On a floured surface, roll dough into a 10-inch circle. Place over filling in pie plate and crimp edge. Chill for 30 minutes.

Cut slits in crust. Bake for 30 minutes or until crust is golden and filling is bubbly.

Remove from oven. Serve slightly warm or cold in dessert dishes.

Yield 8 servings

NOTE: Whipped cream is great with cobbler if you want the extra calories and fat, but don't take seconds! In fact, if you're watching your weight, forget the cream altogether.

NUTRITION FACTS: Serving size-1 Calories 142 Protein 2.5 g. Fiber 2 g. Carbohydrates 24 g. Sugars 12 g. Total Fat 4.5 g. Saturated Fat .75 Sodium 99 mg. Cholesterol .14 mg.

EXCHANGES: Bread .67 Fruit 2

Apple-Nut Crisp

3 or 4 large Yellow or Red Delicious, Fuji, or Gala apples, peeled, cored, and sliced

1/2 cup golden raisins

1/2 cup coarsely chopped walnuts

1 teaspoon apple pie spice or 1/2 teaspoon ground cinnamon and 1/2 teaspoon ground nutmeg (optional)

TOPPING

1/2 cup unsalted margarine or butter, melted

1 tablespoon brown or white sugar substitute or 2 tablespoons granulated fructose

2 cups crushed shredded wheat or crushed shredded wheat and bran squares

1 1/2 tablespoons all-purpose flour

1/2 cup coarsely chopped walnuts

Layer about a third of the apple slices on the bottom of an 8- or 9-inch pie plate. Sprinkle with spice, half of the raisins, and half of the walnuts. Repeat for the second layer and then top with the rest of the apple slices.

For the topping, pour melted margarine into a small bowl. Stir in sugar substitute of your choice.

In a bowl, whisk together the crushed shredded wheat, flour, and walnuts. Add the melted mixture and mix with your hands until well coated. Spread evenly over the top of the apples.

Preheat oven to 350° and bake for 60 minutes or until apples are done and top is browned. Do not overcook apples. The top will be crispy-crunchy. Serve warm or cold.

Makes 8 to 10 servings

NOTE: This is one of my favorite recipes. I'm sure that you will add it to your "most often baked" list also. I prefer it without spice in the filling.

NUTRITION FACTS: Serving size-1 Calories 307 Protein 4 g. Fiber 4 g. Carbohydrates 29.5 g. Sugars 15.5 g. Total Fat 21 g. Saturated Fat 3 g. Sodium 139 mg. Cholesterol 0 mg.

EXCHANGES: Bread .69 Fruit 1

Blueberry Crisp

3 cups fresh or frozen unsweetened blueberries

3 tablespoons all-purpose flour

3 tablespoons sugar substitute or 2/3 cup granulated fructose

2 tablespoons lemon juice

1 1/2 cups crumbled shredded wheat squares or biscuits

3 teaspoons (9 packets) sugar substitute or 2 tablespoons granulated fructose

1 teaspoon ground cinnamon

1 tablespoon all-purpose flour

3 tablespoons melted margarine or butter

Preheat oven to 350°. Lightly butter or oil spray an 8-inch round cake pan or ovenproof dish.

If using fresh berries, pick over carefully for stems. In a colander, wash berries, drain well, and pat almost dry with a paper towel. In a bowl, dredge berries in 3 tablespoons of flour. If using frozen berries, dredge the same way. Mix in sugar substitute. Add lemon juice and gently stir together. Spoon the berry mixture into the prepared pan.

In a small bowl, combine the shredded wheat, sugar substitute, cinnamon, and flour with the melted margarine. Spread evenly over the blueberries.

Bake for 35 minutes or until cooked and bubbly. The topping should be browned. Do not overbake. Serve warm or cold.

Serves 8

NUTRITION FACTS: Serving size-1 Calories 115 Protein 1.7 g. Fiber 2.5 g. Carbohydrates 18.2 g. Sugars 7g. Total Fat 4.64 g. Saturated Fat .53 g. Sodium 64.8 mg. Cholesterol 0 mg.

EXCHANGES: Bread .5 Fruit .5 Fat .8

Apple-Raisin Pie with Walnuts

Dough for single-crust pie or ready-made crust (no sugar)
3 or 4 large sweet apples (Golden Delicious or Fuji)
1 1/2 teaspoons apple pie spice or 1 teaspoon ground cinnamon and
    1/2 teaspoon ground nutmeg
1/2 cup golden raisins
1/2 cup coarsely chopped walnuts
1 tablespoon margarine or butter

Preheat oven at 375°. Set aside an 8- or 9-inch metal or glass ovenproof pie plate.

Roll out dough 3 inches larger than the pie plate. Place dough gently in the plate, letting the edges hang over.

Core, peel, and slice the apples (not too thin) and arrange one-third of them on the crust. Sprinkle a little spice on top, and add half the raisins, half the nuts, and a few dabs of margarine. Add half the remaining apples and repeat the process above, using the rest of the toppings. Form a mound with the last layer of apples and fold the pie crust up around them, crimping where needed, to form a large open tart.

You will need a large sheet of aluminum foil or a lightweight aluminum pie plate to cover the pie as it bakes (I always keep a disposable deep-dish pie plate on hand to cover my one-crust pies.) Pierce many holes into the pie plate with an ice pick or awl. If you use foil, punch holes in it before covering the pie. Place pie plate or foil over the top of the pie and bake for 40 to 55 minutes. Place a piece of foil on the oven rack under the pie in case it bubbles over. Check the pie after 30 minutes. If the apples are pretty well cooked, uncover the pie if the crust needs browning on the edges. Bake until edges are brown, but do not let the apples dry up.

Serves 8

NUTRITION FACTS: Serving size-1 Calories 319 Protein 4 g. Fiber 3 g. Carbohydrates 34 g. Sugars 14 g. Total Fat 19 g. Saturated Fat 4 g. Sodium 152 mg. Cholesterol 0 mg.

EXCHANGES: Bread 1 Fat 2.5

Banana Cream Pie with Chocolate and Nuts

9-inch prebaked pie crust, thoroughly cooled

5 tablespoons cornstarch

4 tablespoons all-purpose flour

3 cups low-fat milk

3 egg yolks

3 teaspoons (9 packets) sugar substitute or 5 tablespoons granulated fructose

1 teaspoon butter (optional)

1 teaspoon vanilla extract

1 teaspoon almond extract

2 ripe bananas

1/4 cup coarsely chopped walnuts

CHOCOLATE CRUMBLES

2 ounces (2 squares) unsweetened baking chocolate

1 1/2 teaspoons (5 packets) sugar substitute or 3 teaspoons granulated fructose

1 teaspoon cream

Buy a ready-made pie crust or bake a single pie crust (page 20).

In a small bowl, mix cornstarch, flour, and 1/2 cup of the milk. Whisk together until smooth. Transfer to a medium-size saucepan. Add remaining milk and egg yolks. Whisk together and cook over medium heat, stirring constantly, until mixture boils. Quickly reduce heat, continue to stir, and cook for 5 minutes more. Pudding should be thick. Stir in sugar substitute and remove from heat. Stir in butter, and vanilla, and almond extracts. Do a taste test and add more sweetener if needed. Set aside to cool slightly. The pudding will thicken when cooled.

For the chocolate crumbles, chop or cut the chocolate squares into smaller pieces and place in a small custard cup. Add the sugar substitute and microwave on high for 25 to 45 seconds or until melted. Watch carefully. When melted, mix well and quickly stir in the cream. The chocolate will start to stiffen. With a fork, crumble the chocolate. Set aside.

On a large plate, slice the bananas down the center and cut into 2-inch chunks. Mix the walnuts and half of the chocolate crumbles into the pudding. Spoon about two-thirds of it into the pie crust. Arrange the banana pieces in the pudding so that they are evenly spaced and well coated. Spoon in and spread out the rest of the pudding, making sure that all the bananas are covered. Sprinkle the rest of the crumbled chocolate on top.

Serves 10

NOTE: Adding chopped walnuts and chocolate crumbles to a plain banana cream pie really perks it up. I think you will enjoy this combination for a change from the ordinary.

NUTRITION FACTS: Serving size-1 Calories 220 Protein 5.74 g. Fiber 1.84 g. Carbohydrates 23.5 g. Sugars 8.4 g. Total Fat 12.24 g. Saturated Fat 4.04 g. Sodium 123.6 mg. Cholesterol 69.6 mg.

EXCHANGES: Bread .4 Carbohydrates .6 Lean Meat .2 Fruit .4 Milk .3 Fat 2.2

Blueberry Cream Pie

9-inch prebaked pie crust, thoroughly cooled

5 tablespoons cornstarch

4 tablespoons all-purpose flour

3 cups low-fat milk

3 egg yolks

5 tablespoons granulated fructose or 3 teaspoons (8 packets) sugar substitute

1 teaspoon vanilla extract

1 teaspoon almond extract

2 cups fresh blueberries

1 tablespoon granulated fructose or 2 packets sugar substitute

1 teaspoon all-purpose flour

Buy a ready-made pie crust or bake a single pie crust (page 20).

In a small bowl, mix cornstarch, flour, and 1/2 cup of the milk. Whisk together until smooth. Transfer to a saucepan. Add remainder of milk and egg yolks. Whisk together and cook over medium heat, stirring constantly, until mixture boils. Quickly reduce heat, continue to stir, and cook for 5 minutes more. Pudding should be thick. Stir in fructose. Remove from heat. Stir in vanilla and almond extracts. Do a taste test and add more sweetener if needed. Set aside to cool slightly. The pudding will thicken when cooled.

In a bowl, add 1 cup blueberries, fructose, and flour. Stir together gently with a large spoon. Microwave on high for 45 seconds. Remove from microwave oven. Carefully mix in the rest of the berries.

Spoon half of the pudding into the pie crust. Lightly place half of the blueberries evenly on top of the pudding. Repeat for the second layer. When the pie is thoroughly cooled, cover with plastic wrap and chill for 2 hours or more. Try not to let the plastic wrap touch the filling because it will stick to it and make it messy. Try covering it with an inverted pie plate that fits tightly.

Serves 10

NUTRITION FACTS: Serving size-1 Calories 187 Protein 4.35 g. Fiber 1.03 g. Carbohydrates 25.5 g. Sugars 7.1 g. Total Fat 7.23 g. Saturated Fat 2 g. Sodium 122.7 mg. Cholesterol 69.3 mg.

EXCHANGES: Bread .4 Carbohydrates .4 Fruit .3 Milk .3 Fat 1.3

No-Bake Mocha Cream Cheese Dessert

1 1/2 ounces (1 1/2 squares) unsweetened chocolate, chopped
2 packets sugar substitute or 2 teaspoons granulated fructose
1 tablespoon unflavored gelatin (1 envelope)
1/4 cup strong coffee, warm
1 cup (8 ounces) low-fat cream cheese, at room temperature
5 tablespoons granulated fructose
2 tablespoons sugar substitute or 4 tablespoons granulated fructose
1 teaspoon vanilla extract
2 large eggs, separated
1 tablespoon orange zest (optional)
1/4 teaspoon cream of tartar
2/3 cup whipping cream

In a custard cup, mix the chocolate with 2 packets of sugar substitute. Melt in microwave oven. Watch it carefully. Cool slightly and set aside. In a cup, dissolve gelatin in coffee. Set aside.

In a bowl, using electric mixer on slow to medium speed, beat together cream cheese, fructose, sugar substitute, and vanilla until smooth. Beat in egg yolks, one at a time. Beat in chocolate and then gelatin mixture.

Increase speed and beat until very smooth. Add orange zest. (Try it. It adds a delicious flavor.) Do a taste test and add more sweetener if needed.

In a very clean small bowl, beat egg whites until soft peaks form. Add cream of tartar and beat until stiff peaks form. Fold into the cream cheese mixture. In another small bowl, whip the cream until it forms soft peaks. Gently fold into the mixture. Pour into individual dessert dishes. Chill several hours or overnight.

Serves 8

NOTE: This recipe can also be poured into a prebaked pie crust and chilled to make a wonderful pie, but the pie crust is not included in the Facts and Exchanges.

NUTRITION FACTS: Serving size-1 Calories 210 Protein 6.6 g. Fiber .8 g. Carbohydrates 10.5 g. Sugars 2.8 g. Total Fat 16.5 g. Saturated Fat 9.8 g. Sodium 110 mg. Cholesterol 95.8 mg.

EXCHANGES: Lean Meat .62 Milk .14 Fat 3

Chocolate-Raspberry
Cream Cheese Pie

TOPPING AND CRUST

- 1 1/4 cups all-purpose flour
- 1/2 cup unsweetened cocoa powder
- 1 teaspoon baking powder
- (4 packets) sugar substitute
- 5 tablespoons granulated fructose or 3/4 cup fructose and no sugar substitute
- 1/2 cup tub margarine or butter, melted
- 1/3 cup pecans, walnuts, or sliced blanched almonds, chopped medium to fine
- 2 tablespoons real sour cream or plain cream yogurt
- 2 tablespoons seedless all-fruit raspberry jam (no sugar)

FILLING

- 1 cup (8 ounces) cream cheese, softened
- 1/4 cup egg substitute or 1 egg, beaten
- 5 packets sugar substitute or 5 tablespoons granulated fructose
- 1/2 cup half-and-half
- 1 teaspoon almond extract
- 1 packet sugar substitute or 1 teaspoon granulated fructose
- 1 cup fresh or frozen raspberries (no sugar)

Preheat oven to 325°. Butter a 9-inch pie pan and set aside.

In a medium bowl, whisk together flour, cocoa, and baking powder. Whisk in sugar substitute and fructose (or fructose only). Stir in melted margarine until flour mixture is crumbly and thoroughly moistened. Reserve 1 cup of mixture for topping. Into remaining mixture, stir in chopped nuts of your choice and sour cream. Mix well and form a ball.

Place ball in prepared pie pan and press dough evenly on bottom and up the sides to the rim. Spread jam over bottom and sides.

In a medium bowl, combine cream cheese, egg substitute, 5 packets sugar substitute, half-and-half, and almond extract. Beat until light and smooth.

In a small bowl, sprinkle 1 packet of sugar substitute over the raspberries and mix gently. If using frozen berries, do not let them thaw. Place whole raspberries evenly over the jam in the pie crust. Pour in the filling and top with remaining berries. Crumble the reserved cup of chocolate mixture over the top for the finishing touch.

Bake for 55 minutes or more, until knife inserted in center comes out almost clean. Do not let filling brown. It will set while cooling. Cool and then cover tightly and refrigerate for at least 2 hours.

Serves 16

NOTE: This recipe is rich, divine, and decadent. Cut very small pieces. You will need a great deal of control to refuse seconds!

NUTRITION FACTS: Serving size-1 Calories 140 Protein .24 g. Fiber .90 g. Carbohydrates 9.8 g. Sugars 1g. Total Fat 10.4 g. Saturated Fat 2 g. Sodium 106 mg. Cholesterol 17 mg.

EXCHANGES: Bread .50 Fat 2

Tangy Lemon Meringue Pie

7 tablespoons cornstarch

1 1/2 cups warm water

3 eggs, separated

2 tablespoons margarine or butter

1/2 cup granulated fructose or 12 packets sugar substitute

1 teaspoon thinly sliced and snipped or grated lemon zest

1/2 cup fresh lemon juice

9-inch prebaked pie crust, thoroughly cooled

1/4 teaspoon cream of tartar

1/2 teaspoon fructose (optional)

Preheat oven to 350°.

In a 3-cup saucepan, mix cornstarch with just enough cold water to allow you to stir it together until smooth. Gradually stir in warm water and cook over direct medium heat, stirring constantly until thick and clear. Remove from heat and cool slightly. Beat egg yolks well. Set whites aside. Stir half of the cornstarch mixture into yolks, mix, and pour into the saucepan. Cook over low heat 2 to 3 minutes, stirring constantly. Stir in margarine and remove from heat. Add 1/2 cup fructose, lemon zest, and juice. Stir until smooth. While hot, do a taste test. Add more sweetener or lemon juice if needed, but not too much. Filling should be thick. Cool slightly and then pour into pie crust.

Beat egg whites until frothy. Add cream of tartar, beat, and gradually add 1/2 teaspoon fructose, beating until meringue stands in firm, glossy peaks. Spread meringue on cooled filling, making sure it touches inner edge of crust around pie. If it does not touch, it will shrink away while baking.

Bake for 15 minutes or until delicately browned. Cool and then chill before serving.

Serves 8

NUTRITION FACTS: Serving size-1 Calories 333 Protein 5 g. Fiber .76 g.
Carbohydrates 39 g. Sugars 14 g. Total Fat 17 g. Saturated Fat 4 g.
Sodium 193 mg. Cholesterol 79 mg.

EXCHANGES: Bread 1.37 Meat .37 Fruit 1 Fat 2.78

Pumpkin Pie with Orange Zest

1/2 cup egg substitute or 2 eggs, beaten
2 tablespoons granulated fructose
1/2 teaspoon salt (optional)
1 tablespoon pumpkin pie spice
1 3/4 cups canned or cooked pumpkin (no sugar added)
1 1/2 cups low-fat milk or 3/4 cup evaporated milk diluted with
   3/4 cup water
1 tablespoon sliced and snipped orange zest
Unbaked 9-inch pie shell

Preheat oven to 425°.

In a large bowl, combine egg substitute, fructose, salt, and spice. Add
pumpkin and mix. Stir in the milk. Taste for sweetness. If you think it needs
a little more fructose, add just a little more. Mix in the orange zest.

Pour mixture into the pie shell. Protect the crust with strips of foil until
the last 10 minutes. Bake for 40 minutes or until a knife inserted in center
comes out clean. Remove from oven and cool. Pie will continue to set while
cooling.

Serves 8

NOTE: Substitute cooked mashed winter squash or yams in place of pumpkin. Mashed red yams are my favorite. Try these substitutes at different
times, based on what is in season. They all make great pies. Before serving,
whip up a bowl of cream without sugar or provide a sugar-free topping for

those who might enjoy a dollop on their slice. For a festive holiday pie, spread a thin layer of Cranberry-Orange Sauce (page 114) on top of the pie and pile some whipped cream or topping in the center. These additions are not for strict dieters, but for others, they make colorful, tasty additions. Changes to the original recipe are not included in the Facts and Exchanges.

NUTRITION FACTS: Serving size-1 Calories 271. Protein 6 g. Fiber 2 g. Carbohydrates 27 g. Sugars 8 g. Total Fat 16 g. Saturated Fat 4 g. Sodium 454 mg. Cholesterol 3.7 mg.

EXCHANGES: Bread 1 Meat .25 Fruit .25 Milk .19 Fat 2.8

Quick Pudding Pie

Single unbaked pie shell, homemade or store-bought
1 large (2 ounce) package sugar-free vanilla, chocolate, butterscotch,
   or pistachio pudding (cook and serve or instant)
1/4 cup chopped walnuts

Preheat oven to 350°. With fork tines, prick many holes in the bottom and sides of the pie shell. Bake pie shell until crispy and golden. Remove from oven and cool.

Follow directions to prepare sugar-free pudding of your choice. If you are using pudding that must be cooked, add the nuts toward the end of the cooking time and let the pudding cool. Spoon the pudding into the cooled pie shell. Cover tightly so that a skin does not form on the pudding. Refrigerate and chill 3 hours or overnight.

Serves 8

NOTE: If desired, prepare a bowl of whipped cream (without sugar) or use sugar-free whipped topping. Extras are not included in Facts or Exchanges.

NUTRITION FACTS: Serving size-1 Calories 127 Protein 2.29 g. Fiber .68 g. Carbohydrates 13.45 g. Sugars .17 g. Total Fat 7.39 g. Saturated Fat .92 g. Sodium 314.9 mg. Cholesterol 0 mg.

EXCHANGES: Carbohydrates 1.2 Lean Meat .1 Fat 1.4

Fresh Strawberry Pie

7 1/2 cups fresh whole strawberries
1 1/2 tablespoons sugar substitute or 3 tablespoons granulated
    fructose
2 1/2 tablespoons cornstarch
1 teaspoon sugar substitute or granulated fructose for whole berries
1 prebaked single pie crust, cooled

In a bowl, cut and mash enough strawberries to equal 1 1/2 cups. Save large berries for topping. Stir in 1 1/2 tablespoons of sugar substitute. Spoon out 1/2 cup of the strawberry juice. Some pulp may be in the juice, but that's okay. Add the cornstarch to the juice, mix, and stir until smooth, making sure that there are no lumps.

In a nonstick saucepan, combine the strawberry pulp and the cornstarch mixture and cook over medium heat for 5 minutes or more, stirring constantly. Bring to a boil until thickened; it will change from a milky color to clear. Let cool slightly.

In another bowl, lightly toss the rest of the large whole strawberries with 1 teaspoon of sugar substitute.

When strawberry mixture is slightly cooled, spoon into the cooled baked pie crust. Spread out evenly. Push the whole berries into the pie in a decorative arrangement.

Serves 8

NOTE: This pie has "eye appeal" and is delicious! Offer a small bowl of plain whipped cream to the guests who can't resist adding a spoonful to top it off. Take advantage of fresh strawberry season and make this one often. It's easy to make and sure to please everyone!

NUTRITION FACTS: Serving size-1 Calories 223 Protein 2.7 g. Fiber 2 g. Carbohydrates 24 g. Sugars 2.8 g. Total Fat 13 g. Saturated Fat 3 g. Sodium 136 mg. Cholesterol I 0 mg.x

EXCHANGES: Bread 1 Fruit .22 Fat 2.5

Sweet Potato–Cream Cheese Pie

1 cup red yams, mashed
1 cup finely crushed shredded wheat
1 teaspoon brown sugar substitute or granulated fructose
1/4 cup melted margarine or butter
1 cup (8 ounces) nonfat cream cheese, at room temperature
6 teaspoons granulated fructose or 1 tablespoon sugar substitute
1/4 cup heavy or whipping cream
1 teaspoon vanilla extract
1 teaspoon pumpkin pie spice
1/2 cup egg substitute or 2 eggs
1/2 cup coarsely chopped walnuts
1 teaspoon thinly sliced and snipped or grated orange zest

Preheat oven to 350°. Cook, drain, and finely mash or purée yams. This can be done the day before or early enough for it to cool.

For the pie shell, place shredded wheat, sugar substitute, and margarine in an 8- or 9-inch pie plate and mix together thoroughly. Press with a spoon to cover bottom and sides. Always prepare your crust before mixing the filling so that it will be ready to fill.

In a large bowl, cut cream cheese into small pieces. Add fructose or sugar substitute (sometimes I use half of each). With electric mixer, beat on low to medium until creamed together. Add the cream, vanilla, pumpkin pie spice, and half of the egg substitute or 1 egg, beating at medium speed. Add the rest of the egg substitute or second egg. Beat and gradually add the mashed yams. Beat well. Do the taste test. Add more sweetener if needed. Stir in the walnuts and orange zest.

Bake for approximately 1 hour or until knife inserted in center comes out clean and the pie is set. Cool completely and chill before serving.

Serves 8

NOTE: An ice-cold pie will yield 12 thin slices. Because this pie is rich and creamy, a small slice is sufficient and will lower your Facts and Exchanges, unless you decide to top it with plain whipped cream. Which would you rather do?

NUTRITION FACTS: Serving size 1 Calories 234 Protein 8 g. Fiber 2 g. Carbohydrates 18 g. Sugars 5 g. Total Fat 15 g. Saturated Fat 3 g. Sodium 246 mg. Cholesterol 10.5 mg.

EXCHANGES: Bread .65 Lean Meat .25 Fat .65

REMEMBER: To prevent bitter-tasting desserts, never bake or boil Equal or NutraSweet.

ABOUT THE FACTS AND EXCHANGES: Ingredients marked as "optional" are included. When the ingredients list offers alternatives (i.e., sugar substitute or fructose), figures are based on the first item listed. Sugar grams are always included in the total carbohydrate counts, in addition to being shown separately.

CHAPTER 5

DECORATE YOUR DESSERTS

Fluffy Cream Cheese Frosting

1 cup (8 ounces) nonfat cream cheese, at room temperature
1 tablespoon skim milk
1 teaspoon vanilla or other flavored extract of your choice
2 1/2 teaspoons sugar substitute or 5 tablespoons granulated fructose
1 1/2 cups light whipped topping or use nonfat Cool Whip and
    eliminate the sugar substitute or fructose

In a medium bowl, cut cream cheese into small pieces. Add milk, vanilla, and sugar substitute. Beat together until creamy and smooth. Whisk or beat in your choice of topping.

NUTRITION FACTS: Whole Recipe Calories 481 Protein 34 g. Fiber 0 g. Carbohydrates 38.8 g. Sugars 12.8 g. Total Fat 15.2 g. Saturated Fat 14.1 g. Sodium 1273 mg. Cholesterol 18.87 mg.

EXCHANGES: Bread .9 Lean Meat 4.6 Milk .1 Fat 2.4

Cream Cheese Topping or Filling

6 tablespoons low-fat cream cheese, at room temperature

2 tablespoons unsweetened fruit juice concentrate of your choice

1 teaspoon sugar substitute or 1 tablespoon granulated fructose (optional)

1/4 teaspoon flavored extract of your choice: vanilla, almond, lemon, orange, rum, etc. (optional)

1/8 teaspoon ground cinnamon or ground nutmeg (optional)

In a small bowl, beat together cream cheese and juice concentrate until very smooth. Taste for sweetness. Add some sweetener if necessary. You can also use an extract and/or a spice to flavor the topping. Mix well before using in the recipe of your choice.

NOTE: Depending on what you have baked, you may want to make a larger quantity of this recipe to fill a cake and frost it also. The amount you need will depend on how thick you spread it on. Try adding fresh sliced fruit over a thin layer of topping, placing the fruit in a decorative design. Try topping it off with chopped nuts or unsweetened flaked coconut. Perhaps you'd like to use some grated or thinly sliced orange zest or grated bittersweet chocolate. There are so many different ways to add the finishing touch to your dessert. Try different combinations and be creative!

The variety of extra choices suggested are not included in Facts and Exchanges. For one serving of topping, divide the individual Facts and Exchange quantities by the number of servings listed for the recipe you made. Add to the numbers in Facts and Exchanges for that recipe to get the total.

NUTRITION FACTS: Whole Recipe Calories 272 Protein 10.23 g. Fiber .34 g. Carbohydrates 21.5 g. Sugars 20.41 g. Total Fat 16 g. Saturated Fat 10 g. Sodium 278 mg. Cholesterol 50.4 mg.

EXCHANGES: Bread .4 Lean Meat 1.2 Fruit .9 Fat 2.4

Creamy Frosting

1 cup (8 ounces) nonfat cream cheese, at room temperature
1/4 cup light cream
2 teaspoons sugar substitute or 4 tablespoons granulated fructose
1 teaspoon vanilla or almond extract
1 teaspoon sliced and snipped or grated orange or lemon zest (optional)

In a medium bowl, cut softened cream cheese into pieces. Add all other ingredients. Beat by hand or use electric mixer set on low to medium. Mix until creamy. Test for sweetness and add more sweetener if necessary. If too thick, add more light cream.

NUTRITION FACTS: Whole Recipe Calories 363 Protein 38.2 g. Fiber .21 g. Carbohydrates 22.3 g. Sugars 9.89 g. Total Fat 11.6 g. Saturated Fat 7.2 g. Sodium 1263.3 mg. Cholesterol 62.5 mg.

EXCHANGES: Lean Meat 9.1 Milk .2 Fat 2.3

Creamy Chocolate Frosting

1 cup (8 ounces) nonfat or regular cream cheese, at room temperature

3 tablespoons nonfat plain yogurt

7 tablespoons unsweetened cocoa powder

2 teaspoons cornstarch

4 teaspoons (12 packets) sugar substitute or 7 tablespoons granulated fructose

8 tablespoons water

2 teaspoons vanilla extract

1 teaspoon grated orange zest (optional)

In a medium bowl, cut cream cheese in pieces. Cream together with yogurt.

In a small bowl, mix together cocoa, cornstarch, and sugar substitute. Add the water and vanilla. Mix until smooth. Taste for sweetness and add sweetener to suit your preference.

Gradually add the cocoa mixture to the cream cheese. With a small whisk or fork, beat thoroughly. Using a spatula, scrape the sides and bottom of the bowl to make sure the frosting is evenly mixed. Stir in the orange zest.

Makes enough to frost an 8-inch layer cake

NOTE: If you are a nut lover like I am, top your frosting off with chopped walnuts. The walnuts are not included in the Facts and Exchanges.

NUTRITION FACTS: Whole Recipe Calories 397 Protein 46.7 g. Fiber 13.2 g. Carbohydrates 51.2 g. Sugars 14.9 g. Total Fat 5.3 g. Saturated Fat 3.1 g. Sodium 1292 mg. Cholesterol 23.68 mg.

EXCHANGES: Bread 1.2 Carbohydrates .1 Lean Meat 9.1 Fruit .1 Milk .3 Fat .5

Fruity Cream Cheese Topping

6 tablespoons nonfat cream cheese, at room temperature

2 tablespoons seedless, all-fruit jam, jelly, or spreadable fruit
   (no sugar added), any flavor

1 teaspoon or more of cream if needed

In small or medium bowl, cut cream cheese into small pieces and beat with electric mixer until smooth. Add the jam you have chosen and beat into cream cheese or swirl it in by hand. Do the taste test to see if it has enough flavor for you, and add some more jam if necessary. If the mixture is too thick, add a teaspoon or more of cream to thin it to a good consistency for spreading.

   NOTE: Use this spread on crepes. Top your cheesecake with it. Use as a spread on muffins instead of butter. Fill and top a layer cake. Add nuts or fruit over the topping if desired.

NUTRITION FACTS: Whole Recipe Calories 150 Protein 15.14 g. Fiber 1 g. Carbohydrates 18.2 g. Sugars 14 g. Total Fat .97 g. Saturated Fat .60 g. Sodium 487 mg. Cholesterol 10.8 mg.

EXCHANGES: Carbohydrates 1 Fat .2

Chocolate Sauce

2 tablespoons unsweetened cocoa powder

2 tablespoons cornstarch

3/4 cup water

2 tablespoons nonfat cream cheese, at room temperature

2 teaspoons vanilla extract

2 teaspoons sugar substitute or 4 tablespoons granulated fructose

In a small saucepan, whisk together cocoa and cornstarch. Add water. Mix until smooth. Add cream cheese and beat in with wire whisk. Cook over medium heat. Whisk constantly until thickened and smooth. Remove from heat. Whisk in vanilla. Whisk in sugar substitute gradually because you may want to use less. Taste before adding all of it. If it needs more, adjust accordingly.

NUTRITION FACTS: Whole recipe Calories 141 Protein 6.3 g. Fiber 3.71 g. Carbohydrates 24 g. Sugars 1 g. Total Fat 1.88 g. Saturated Fat 1.13 g. Sodium 172.6 mg. Cholesterol 2.32 mg.

EXCHANGES: Bread 1.4 Lean Meat .6 Fat .1

Cranberry-Orange Sauce

1 tablespoon cornstarch (optional)
1/2 cup orange juice concentrate
1 1/2 or 2 cups fresh cranberries
1/4 cup sugar substitute or 1/2 cup granulated fructose
1 tablespoon sliced and snipped or grated orange zest (optional)

In a cup, mix cornstarch in a small amount of orange juice concentrate until smooth. Mix in the rest of the concentrate and pour into a medium saucepan. Add cranberries and sugar substitute. Cook on high to medium heat. Adjust your heat, stir often, and cook until cranberries pop and sauce has thickened. Remove from stove and stir in zest. Do a taste test and add more sweetener if needed.

NUTRITION FACTS: Whole recipe Calories 349 Protein 4.06 g. Fiber 7.83 g. Carbohydrates 85.7 g. Sugars 69.7 g. Total Fat .60 g. Saturated Fat .06 g. Sodium 35.39 mg. Cholesterol 0 mg.

EXCHANGES: Bread .5 Carbohydrates .3 Fruit 4.8

Lemon Sauce

3/4 cup water
2 teaspoons sugar substitute or 2 tablespoons granulated fructose
2 tablespoons cornstarch
1/4 cup fresh lemon juice
1 tablespoon thinly sliced and snipped or grated lemon zest
2 tablespoons butter or margarine

Pour water into a small saucepan. If using a sugar substitute, set aside and add after sauce is cooked. If using fructose, add to saucepan. In a cup, mix cornstarch with just enough water to make a smooth paste with no lumps. Gradually stir into saucepan.

Cook over medium heat, stirring constantly. When sauce thickens and comes to a boil, stir and boil for 1 minute or until it looks clear. Remove from heat. If you are using sugar substitute, mix into saucepan with lemon juice, zest, and butter. Taste for sweetness and, if necessary, stir in more sugar substitute or fructose.

Makes about 1 1/4 cups

NUTRITION FACTS: Whole Recipe Calories 285 Protein .60 g. Fiber 1.02 g. Carbohydrates 21.6 g. Sugars 2.84 g. Total Fat 23 g. Saturated Fat 14.3 g. Sodium 247 mg. Cholesterol 62 mg.

EXCHANGES: Whole Recipe Fruit 0.3 Bread 1.1 Fat 4.6

Orange Sauce

2 tablespoons cornstarch
1 tablespoon all-purpose flour
3 teaspoons sugar substitute or 2 tablespoons granulated fructose
1/2 cup water
1 1/4 cups orange juice
1 tablespoon very thinly sliced or grated orange zest
1 tablespoon butter or margarine

In a small saucepan, mix together cornstarch and flour. If using sugar substitute, set aside and add after sauce is cooked. If using fructose, add to saucepan. Gradually stir in water and orange juice, mixing so that there are no lumps. Bring to a boil over medium to low heat, stirring constantly. Boil and stir 3 more minutes. Remove from heat and stir in orange zest, butter, and sugar substitute if using. Taste for sweetness. Add more sweetener if needed. This sauce is best served warm.

Makes about 2 1/4 cups

NUTRITION FACTS: Whole recipe Calories 341 Protein 3.17 g. Fiber 1.61 g. Carbohydrates 56.8 g. Sugars 34.3 g. Total Fat 11.8 g. Saturated Fat 7.2 Sodium 133 mg. Cholesterol 31.1 mg.

EXCHANGES: Bread 1.4 Carbohydrates .1 Fruit 2.3 Fat 2.3

Flavored Sweetened Whipped Cream

FOR 2 CUPS:

> 1 cup whipping cream *or* heavy cream
> 2 packets sugar substitute *or* 1 tablespoon granulated fructose

Choose a flavoring from the list below. Pour cream and sugar substitute into a very clean bowl. Add flavoring and beat until stiff peaks form. Serve immediately.

FOR 1 CUP:

> 1/2 cup whipping cream *or* heavy cream
> 1 packet sugar substitute *or* 1/2 teaspoon granulated fructose

Choose a flavoring from the list below, but use half the amount listed. Pour cream and sugar substitute into a very clean bowl. Add flavoring and beat until stiff peaks form. Serve immediately.

FLAVORINGS:

> 1 teaspoon grated orange or lemon zest
> 1/2 teaspoon ground nutmeg
> 1/2 teaspoon ground cinnamon
> 1/2 teaspoon ground ginger
> 1 teaspoon vanilla extract
> 1/2 teaspoon almond extract
> 1/2 teaspoon peppermint extract
> 1/2 teaspoon orange extract
> 1/2 teaspoon lemon extract
> 1/4 teaspoon rum flavoring
> 1/4 teaspoon maple flavoring
> 1/4 teaspoon chocolate flavoring

NOTE: Use flavored whipped cream to fill your cream puffs made with Basic Chou Pastry (page 22). Use on puddings, applesauce, fruit, cakes, and pies. Facts and Exchanges are based on the whole 2-cup recipe. For 1 serving, divide the numbers by the servings used in the recipe. For 1 cup, divide Facts and Exchange numbers by 2 and then divide the numbers by the number of servings in the recipe used. This will give you the breakdown for 1 serving. These numbers must then be added to the Facts and Exchange numbers in the recipe used.

NUTRITIONAL FACTS: Whole Recipe Calories 415 Protein 2.44 g. Fiber 0 g. Carbohydrates 4.32 g. Sugars 3.32 g. Total Fat 44 g. Saturated Fat 27 g. Sodium 45 mg. Cholesterol 163 mg.

EXCHANGES: Fat 8.5

REMEMBER: To prevent bitter-tasting desserts, never bake or boil Equal or NutraSweet.

ABOUT THE FACTS AND EXCHANGES: Ingredients marked as "optional" are included. When the ingredients list offers alternatives (i.e., sugar substitute or fructose), figures are based on the first item listed. Sugar grams are always included in the total carbohydrate counts, in addition to being shown separately.

CHAPTER 6

DESSERT BREADS, MUFFINS, AND SCONES

Banana-Nut Bread

3 cups all-purpose flour or 4 cups flour and no oat bran or
   wheat flour

1/2 cup oat bran or wheat flour

2 tablespoons sugar substitute or 5 tablespoons granulated fructose

2 teaspoons baking soda

1/2 cup egg substitute or 2 eggs, beaten

4 large or 6 small ripe bananas, mashed (if not ripe enough, soften in
   microwave)

1/2 cup canola or olive oil

2 teaspoons vanilla extract or 1 teaspoon vanilla and 1 teaspoon
   almond extracts

1 cup coarsely chopped walnuts

1 tablespoon peeled and snipped or grated orange zest (optional)

Preheat oven to 350°. Oil spray a 12-cup bundt pan (my preference) or 9 x
9 x 2-inch baking pan, or rub the sides and bottom with unsalted margarine.

In a medium bowl, whisk together the flour, oat bran, sugar substitute,
and baking soda. Set aside.

In a large bowl, beat together egg substitute, bananas, oil, and vanilla.
The mixing can be done by hand or with an electric mixer on slow to
medium speed. (I like to mix by hand, but that means the baked texture is
not as smooth.) Add the dry ingredients and beat thoroughly. Stir in walnuts and orange zest by hand.

The batter will be thick, so be sure to spread it evenly in the pan. Bake
for 40 minutes, or until knife inserted in center comes out clean. If needed,
bake a little longer, but do not overbake, or the bread will dry out.

A bundt pan will yield 28 slices

NOTE: To make this bread even tastier, add 1/2 cup of fresh or frozen blueberries (no sugar added) after all the other ingredients are mixed. Banana Nut Bread keeps well and freezes well. You can freeze a whole loaf or freeze slices and use as needed. Extras are not included in Facts and Exchanges.

NUTRITION FACTS: Serving size-1 Calories 135 Protein 3.47 g. Fiber 1.3 g. Carbohydrates 16 g. Sugars 3.5 g. Total Fat 6.9 g. Saturated Fat .54 g. Sodium 99 mg. Cholesterol .04 mg.

EXCHANGES: Bread .7 Lean Meat .2 Fruit .3 Fat 1.3

Date-Nut Bread

2 1/2 cups all-purpose flour
1/2 cup oat bran
1/2 cup sugar substitute or 1/2 cup granulated fructose
1 1/2 teaspoons baking powder
1/2 teaspoon baking soda
1/2 cup egg substitute or 2 eggs, beaten
2/3 cup orange juice
2/3 cup water
1/3 cup margarine or butter, melted
2 teaspoons lemon juice or 1 teaspoon lemon extract
1 cup chopped, pitted dates
1 cup coarsely chopped walnuts

Preheat oven to 350°. Butter or oil spray a 9 x 5 x 3-inch loaf pan.

In a large bowl, combine flour, oat bran, sugar substitute, baking powder, and baking soda. Whisk and mix thoroughly. Make a well in the center.

In a bowl, beat together egg substitute, orange juice, water, margarine, and lemon juice. Stir in dates and walnuts and pour into the well in the dry ingredients. Mix with a fork until the dry ingredients are moistened.

Pour ingredients into the prepared pan. Bake for 60 minutes or until a knife inserted into the center comes out clean. Remove from oven and cool 10 minutes. Loosen sides and invert bread on a rack. Serve warm or cold.

Makes 16 thin slices

NOTE: This bread slices better when cold, but is delicious served warm. It will keep for up to a week wrapped in foil. You can also freeze some of it for later use.

NUTRITION FACTS: Serving size-1 Calories 207 Protein 4.7 g. Fiber 2.3 g. Carbohydrates 28 g. Sugars 9 g. Total Fat 9 g. Saturated Fat 1 g. Sodium 148 mg.   Cholesterol .15 mg.

EXCHANGES: Bread 1 Lean Meat .13 Fruit .58 Fat .10

Holiday Pumpkin Bread

1 cup egg substitute or 4 eggs beaten
3/4 cup granulated fructose or 5 teaspoons (16 packets) sugar substitute
1/2 cup canola or vegetable oil
1/2 cup applesauce (no sugar added)
2 cups solid-pack pumpkin (no sugar added)
1/2 cup orange juice with pulp
1 tablespoon sliced and snipped or grated orange zest
1/3 cup or 45 raisins (golden preferred)
1/2 cup coarsely chopped walnuts
3 1/2 cups all-purpose flour
2 teaspoons baking soda
1 teaspoon baking powder
1 teaspoon ground cinnamon
1 teaspoon ground nutmeg
1/4 teaspoon ground cloves
1/2 teaspoon ground allspice

Preheat oven to 350°. Oil a 12-cup bundt pan.

In a large bowl, mix together egg substitute, fructose, oil, and applesauce. Add pumpkin, orange juice, orange zest, raisins, and nuts. Mix well.

In a medium bowl, whisk together the flour, baking soda, baking powder, and spices. Add small amounts of dry ingredients to the wet ingredients. Mix well and scrape sides of bowl each time you add more. Do a taste test for sweetness.

Distribute batter evenly and bake for 50 to 60 minutes or until knife inserted comes out clean. Cool for 10 minutes and invert pan on wire rack to cool thoroughly.

Makes 28 slices

NOTE: This recipe makes a special holiday treat that everyone will love.

NUTRITION FACTS: Serving size-1 Calories 139 Protein 3.4 g. Fiber 1.2 g. Carbohydrates 19.1 g. Sugars 2.9 g. Total Fat 5.7 g. Saturated Fat .49 g. Sodium 124.8 mg. Cholesterol .09 mg.

EXCHANGES: Bread .7 Lean Meat .2 Fruit .2 Fat 1.1

Banana-Oat Muffins

2 cups all-purpose flour
1/3 cup whole-wheat flour
1/3 cup six-grain cereal or rolled oats (not quick cooking oats)
1 teaspoon baking soda
1 1/2 teaspoons baking powder
1 cup mashed ripe bananas (about 3 bananas)
2 tablespoons sugar substitute or granulated fructose
1/4 cup egg substitute or 1 egg, beaten
1/2 cup skim milk
1/4 cup canola oil or melted margarine
1/3 cup golden raisins
1/3 cup coarsely chopped walnuts

Preheat oven to 375°. Spray a 12-cup muffin pan with nonfat cooking spray or use a nonstick pan.

In a large bowl, whisk the flours, cereal, baking soda, and baking powder together thoroughly. Set aside.

On a large plate, mash bananas with a fork. Sprinkle sugar substitute over the bananas and mix together thoroughly. Scrape bananas into a bowl. Add egg substitute, milk, and oil. Mix well. Stir in the raisins and walnuts. Add this mixture to the dry ingredients and stir until completely mixed.

Fill each muffin cup half full and distribute the remaining batter evenly among the muffins. Bake for 20 minutes or until a knife inserted in the center comes out clean. Remove from oven. Cool on rack.

Serves 12

NOTE: You can also use this recipe for 6 large muffins. If you do this, you must remember to double the numbers in the Facts and Exchanges because they are based on one of twelve muffins. These muffins are moist and delicious warm or cold. They can be frozen also. Enjoy!

NUTRITION FACTS: Serving size-1 Calories 194 Protein 5 g. Fiber 2 g. Carbohydrates 28 g. Sugars 7 g. Total Fat 7 g. Saturated Fat .79 g. Sodium 127 mg. Cholesterol .28 mg.

EXCHANGES: Bread 1 Fruit .47 Fat 1

Blueberry Muffins

3/4 cup all-purpose flour

1/4 cup whole-wheat flour

2 teaspoons baking powder

1/4 cup nonfat plain yogurt

1/2 cup strawberry-guava juice or peach, apricot, or orange juice

1/4 cup egg substitute or 1 large egg, beaten

1 tablespoon thinly sliced and snipped or grated lemon or orange zest

3 tablespoons unsalted margarine or butter, melted

2 tablespoons sugar substitute or 5 tablespoons granulated fructose

1/2 cup fresh blueberries, picked over but not washed

Preheat oven to 400°. Oil spray 2 nonstick small 12-section muffin pans or use nonstick pans.

In a bowl, whisk together the flours and baking powder.

In a large bowl, beat together yogurt, juice, egg substitute, zest, melted margarine, and sugar substitute. Stir dry ingredients into the wet mixture until just combined.

Fill each prepared muffin section half full. Push whole berries into the center of each muffin, being careful not to touch the sides. Based on berry size, use three or four per muffin. Finish filling muffin sections. There will be enough batter for 6 muffins in the second pan.

Bake 25 minutes or until knife inserted in center comes out clean. Remove from oven, cool for 5 minutes and transfer from pan to a rack. Serve warm or cool.

Makes 18 small muffins

NOTE: These muffins disappear in a hurry! If you bake a double batch, you might have a few left to freeze individually and use later.

NUTRITION FACTS: Serving size-1 Calories 53 Protein 1.45 g. Fiber .53 g. Carbohydrates 7.3 g. Sugars 1.6 g. Total Fat 2.12 g. Saturated Fat .26 g. Sodium 88.9 mg. Cholesterol .10 mg.

EXCHANGES: Bread .3 Lean Meat .1 Fat .4

Grape Muffins

1 1/3 cup all-purpose flour

1/4 cup reduced-fat Bisquick

3 tablespoons sugar substitute or granulated fructose

1 teaspoon baking powder

30 large red seedless grapes, at room temperature

1 cup low-fat milk

3 tablespoons unsalted margarine or butter, melted or 1/4 cup canola oil

1/3 cup egg substitute or 1 large egg, beaten

1 tablespoon thinly sliced and snipped or grated orange zest

Preheat oven to 400°. Oil a 12-cup muffin pan or use a nonstick pan.

In a large bowl, whisk together the flour, Bisquick, sugar substitute, and baking powder. Set aside. In a small bowl, slice each grape into four pieces. Set aside.

In a bowl, beat together the milk, melted margarine, and egg substitute. Pour liquid mixture into dry ingredients and mix until just combined. Gently mix in cut grapes, distributing evenly.

Fill 10 of the 12 muffin cups one-quarter full. Sprinkle on the zest. (Sliced and snipped zest will give greater flavor than the grated kind.) Finish dividing the rest of batter equally into the muffin cups, covering the zest.

Bake for 25 minutes, or until knife inserted in center comes out clean. Remove from oven. Cool for 5 minutes. Place muffins on rack. Serve warm or cold.

Makes 10 muffins

NOTE: You may think grape muffins are unusual, but you'll also find that they taste great! Be creative and try grapes instead of raisins in other recipes also.

NUTRITION FACTS: Serving size-1 Calories 113 Protein 3 g. Fiber .51 g. Carbohydrates 14 g. Sugars 4 g. Total Fat 5 g. Saturated Fat 1 g. Sodium 100 mg. Cholesterol 2 mg.

EXCHANGES: Bread .38 Fruit .20 Fat 1

Hot Fruit Muffins

1 cup all-purpose flour
1/4 cup whole-wheat flour
1 teaspoon baking powder
1/4 cup egg substitute or 1 egg, beaten
3/4 cup strawberry-guava or apple juice
1/4 cup nonfat milk
3 tablespoons margarine or butter, melted
3 tablespoons sugar substitute or granulated fructose
1/2 cup Golden Delicious or Fuji apples, peeled, cored, and chopped
10 golden raisins, cut in pieces
8 walnut halves, coarsely chopped

Preheat oven to 400°. Oil spray a 12-cup muffin pan or use a nonstick pan.

In a large bowl, whisk the flours and baking powder together thoroughly.

In a bowl, combine egg substitute, juice, milk, margarine, and sugar substitute. Mix well. Add the apples, raisins, and walnuts. Pour the mixture into the dry ingredients. Stir together until just mixed. Do not beat.

Spoon mixture into 6 or 8 of the muffin cups, depending on size desired. Bake for 20 to 30 minutes or until knife inserted in center of muffin comes out clean. Remove from oven and serve warm, or cool on a rack.

Makes 6 to 8

NOTE: These moist, tasty muffins will keep for several days and can be rewarmed in a microwave oven for 15 to 25 seconds. Wrap in a paper napkin before warming. Bake a double batch and freeze muffins individually in foil or sealed plastic bags.

NUTRITION FACTS: Serving size-1 Calories 216 Protein 5 g. Fiber 2 g. Carbohydrates 30 g. Sugars 9 g. Total Fat 8.7 g. Saturated Fat 1.3 g. Sodium 153 mg. Cholesterol .38 mg.

EXCHANGES: Bread 1 Lean Meat .25 Fruit .59 Milk .04 Fat.33

Orange-Nut Muffins

1/2 cup coarsely chopped walnuts
4 cups sifted all-purpose flour
2 teaspoons baking soda
2 teaspoons baking powder
2 cups orange juice
1 cup egg substitute or 4 eggs, beaten
1/2 cup margarine or butter, melted
5 tablespoons sugar substitute or 1 1/4 cups granulated fructose
2 tablespoons thinly sliced and snipped orange zest

Preheat oven to 400°. Spread chopped walnuts in a pie plate. Toast for 5 to 10 minutes until they are lightly browned and crisp. Watch them carefully so that they don't burn. Remove from oven and cool. Leave oven on so it is preheated for the muffins.

In a large bowl, sift together flour, baking soda, and baking powder. Add the cooled walnuts and whisk together. Set aside.

In a medium bowl, beat together orange juice, egg substitute, margarine, sugar substitute, and orange zest. Pour the wet ingredients into the dry ingredients. Mix just until thoroughly combined. Do not overmix.

Oil or oil spray two large 6-section muffin pans and add batter. Bake for 25 to 35 minutes or until knife inserted in center comes out clean. Cool for 5 minutes, remove from pans, and place on rack. Serve warm or cold.

Makes 12 large muffins

NOTE: This recipe can also be prepared in medium-size muffin pans, as long as you adjust the Facts and Exchanges. I like to make 6 medium muffins and use the rest of the batter to make a loaf cake. Decorate the loaf cake by putting walnut halves on top before baking. After the cake is baked, remove from pan and glaze with all-fruit orange marmalade. It's very good this way. Additions not included in Facts and Exchanges.

NUTRITION FACTS: Serving size-1 Calories 204 Protein 5 g. Fiber 1 g. Carbohydrates 26 g. Sugars 3.8 g. Total Fat 9 g. Saturated Fat 1 g. Sodium 217 mg. Cholesterol .27 mg.

EXCHANGES: Bread 1.14 Lean Meat .22 Fruit .23 Fat .13

Persimmon-Spice Muffins

1 cup persimmon purée (2 large persimmons)
1 tablespoon Sugar Twin or 3 tablespoons granulated fructose
2 1/2 cups all-purpose flour
2 teaspoons baking powder
1/2 cup rolled oats or oat bran
1 teaspoon ground cinnamon
1/2 teaspoon ground ginger
1/4 cup egg substitute or 1 egg, beaten
1/2 cup orange juice or 1/2 cup low-fat milk
1/4 cup olive oil or melted margarine
1 cup grated or finely chopped apple
2 ounces (60) golden raisins

Preheat oven to 375°. Oil a 12-cup muffin pan or use a nonstick pan.

Ripe persimmon pulp should be translucent and have a jellylike texture. Be careful to remove the membranes, which can be bitter. Scrape or squeeze pulp from the fruit into a measuring cup. Do not use skin. Beat vigorously and set aside.

In a large bowl, combine the Sugar Twin, flour, baking powder, rolled oats, cinnamon, and ginger and whisk together.

In a medium bowl, mix the persimmon purée, egg substitute, juice, and olive oil together. Add chopped apple and raisins. Pour into dry ingredients and mix until just combined.

Spoon batter evenly into each muffin cup. Bake 30 minutes or more, until knife inserted into the center comes out clean. Cool in pan 5 minutes and then remove. Serve warm or thoroughly cool on a rack.

Serves 12

NOTE: These muffins keep well and taste even better the next day. Freeze some!

NUTRITION FACTS: Serving size-1 Calories 185. Protein 4 g. Fiber 2 g. Carbohydrates 31 g. Sugars 8.8 g. Total Fat 6 g. Saturated Fat .8 g. Sodium 342 mg. Cholesterol .1 mg.

EXCHANGES: Bread 1.27 Lean Meat .08 Fruit .58 Fat 1

Blueberry-Buttermilk Scones

2 cups cake flour
1 1/2 tablespoons granulated fructose
1 teaspoon sugar substitute or 1 tablespoon granulated fructose
2 1/2 teaspoons baking powder
1/2 teaspoon baking soda
1/2 teaspoon salt (optional)
1/4 cup unsalted cold butter, cut into 1/2-inch cubes
1 cup fresh or frozen blueberries, patted dry
1/4 cup egg substitute or 1 egg, beaten
2/3 cup buttermilk or cream yogurt

Preheat oven to 425°. Oil a baking sheet or use a nonstick one. In a large bowl, whisk flour, fructose, sugar substitute, baking powder, baking soda, and salt together. With a pastry blender, two knives, or your fingers, cut or rub in cold butter until mixture resembles coarse crumbs. Gently stir in berries.

In a small bowl, beat together egg substitute and buttermilk. Pour into flour mixture and stir just until dough holds together.

Place dough on lightly floured surface and, with floured hands, shape dough into a ball. Divide dough into eight pieces and transfer to prepared baking sheet. Pat each piece down until they are a half-inch thick. You can also transfer the whole ball onto the sheet and pat into a 1/2-inch-thick circle. Using a plastic serrated knife, cut 8 wedges.

Bake scones for 15 minutes, or until knife inserted in center comes out clean. If using frozen berries, the scones may take longer to bake. Scones may be eaten warm or cold, depending on your preference.

Serves 8

NUTRITION FACTS: Serving size-1 Calories 203 Protein 5 g. Fiber 1.2 g. Carbohydrates 29.6 g. Sugars 3.8 g. Total Fat 7 g. Saturated Fat 4 g. Sodium 9.7 mg. Cholesterol 16 mg.

EXCHANGES: Bread 1.25 Lean Meat .13 Fruit .17 Fat 1

Chocolate Chip Scones

2 cups all-purpose flour
1/3 cup unsweetened cocoa powder
2 1/2 teaspoons baking powder
1/2 teaspoon baking soda
1/2 cup butter or margarine
1/4 cup egg substitute or 1 egg, beaten
1/2 cup plain nonfat yogurt
2 teaspoons (6 packets) sugar substitute or 4 tablespoons granulated
   fructose
1/4 cup low-fat ricotta cheese
1/2 cup small semisweet chocolate chips

Preheat oven to 400°. In a large bowl, whisk together flour, cocoa powder, baking powder, and baking soda. Using two knives or pastry blender, cut in butter until mixture resembles crumbs. Make a well in the center.

In a small bowl, beat together egg substitute, yogurt, sugar substitute, and ricotta cheese. Pour into the well and add chocolate chips. Stir with a fork until just moistened. Drop scones by heaping tablespoons, about two inches apart, onto a large nonstick baking sheet.

Bake 15 to 20 minutes, until lightly browned or until knife inserted in center comes out clean. Place scones on a rack to cool, or serve warm, and the chocolate chips will melt in your mouth.

Makes 12 scones

NUTRITION FACTS: Serving size-1 Calories 194 Protein 4.6 g. Fiber 1.6 g. Carbohydrates 21.4 g. Sugars 5.3 g. Total Fat 10.8 g. Saturated Fat 6.5 Sodium 124 mg. Cholesterol 22.5 mg.

EXCHANGES: Bread .9 Carbohydrate .3 Milk.1 Fat 1.9

Lemon Scones

1 3/4 cups all-purpose flour

1/3 cup sugar substitute or 6 tablespoons granulated fructose

2 teaspoons baking powder

1/4 teaspoon baking soda

1 teaspoon sliced and snipped or grated lemon zest

1/3 cup butter or tub margarine, at room temperature

1/4 cup egg substitute or 1 egg

1 egg yolk

3 tablespoons half-and-half

2 tablespoons fresh lemon juice

Preheat oven to 400°. In a large bowl, whisk together flour, sugar substitute, baking powder, baking soda, and lemon zest. Using two knives or pastry blender, cut in butter until flour mixture looks like coarse crumbs.

In a small bowl, use a fork to beat together egg substitute, egg yolk, half-and-half, and lemon juice. Add to flour mixture. Stir just until moistened.

Place dough on a lightly floured surface. Knead dough 10 to 12 strokes and pat out to a half-inch-thick circle. Cut into 8 wedges or use a cutter to make biscuits. Place 2 inches apart on a large nonstick or ungreased baking sheet. Bake 15 minutes or until golden. Remove from oven. Using a spatula, lift scones or biscuits from baking sheet to a wire rack. Serve warm or cool.

Yields 8

NUTRITION FACTS: Serving size-1 Calories 178 Protein 4.2 g. Fiber .72 g. Carbohydrates 21 g. Sugars 1.5 g. Total Fat 8.6 g. Saturated Fat 5 g. Sodium 254 mg. Cholesterol 48 mg.

EXCHANGES: Bread 1.2 Lean Meat .2 Fat 1.6

REMEMBER: To prevent bitter-tasting desserts, never bake or boil Equal or NutraSweet.

ABOUT THE FACTS AND EXCHANGES: Ingredients marked as "optional" are included. When the ingredients list offers alternatives (i.e., sugar substitute or fructose), figures are based on the first item listed. Sugar grams are always included in the total carbohydrate counts, in addition to being shown separately.

CHAPTER 7

PASTRIES AND PUDDINGS

Compotes with Stone Fruits

6 nectarines, peaches, or plums
1/4 cup water
2 1/2 to 3 packets sugar substitute or 2 tablespoons granulated
    fructose
2 teaspoons quick cooking tapioca

Use "just ripe" fruit of your choice. If fruits are too ripe, they will cook up mushy. Overripe fruits are best used for cooked sauces. Underripe fruit will not be as sweet, but some can be mixed in and sweetened to taste.

Peel your fruit if you desire. (I only peel peaches.) Remove the stones (pits). Slice each piece into about 8 slices. If you want chunky pieces, use 6 slices. In a nonstick pan, combine fruit with water and cook over high heat until mixture comes to a boil. Stir often until fruit starts to produce its own juice, being careful that it doesn't stick and burn. Stir in sugar substitute a little at a time. Do a taste test to see how much is necessary. Stir in and turn heat to medium low.

Place tapioca in a cup. Add enough water to cover and soften. When softened, stir into fruit and mix so that there are no lumps. Cook until tapioca is clear and of jelly consistency. If you think that there is too much juice, increase heat and watch the mixture so that the fruit does not burn. The increased heat will cook down some of the juice. Caution! Do not overcook the fruit or it will become mushy.

Yields 3 cups

NOTE: Fruit compote is delicious spooned over sugar-free yogurt or ice cream. Enjoy the flavor by eating a plain dish of it, or bake tart shells, fill with sugar-free vanilla pudding, and top with a spoonful of compote. Bake shortbread biscuits or pound cake and serve topped with compote and plain whipped cream. A spoonful of compote is also delicious on breakfast cereal. For a different texture, try cooking the compote without tapioca. Facts and Exchanges will change depending on what you make, so learn to adjust them.

NUTRITION FACTS: Whole recipe Calories 283 Protein 4.12 g. Fiber 11.76 g. Carbohydrates 72.87 g. Sugars 52.8 g. Total Fat .53 g. Saturated Fat .06 g. Sodium 7.78 mg. Cholesterol 0 mg.

EXCHANGES: Bread .4 Carbohydrates .1 Fruit 4.1

Apple-Raisin Strudel with Nuts

3 1/2 cups chopped sweet apples
1/2 cup golden raisins
1/2 cup coasely chopped walnuts
1/4 cup dry bread crumbs
1 tablespoon fresh lemon juice
1/4 teaspoon ground nutmeg
8 frozen phyllo sheets, thawed
1/4 cup margarine or butter, melted

Preheat oven to 375°. In a large bowl, mix apples, raisins, nuts, bread crumbs, lemon juice, and nutmeg. Set aside.

Fold one thawed phyllo sheet in half crosswise and brush with melted margarine. Keep remaining phyllo covered with a damp, clean dish towel to prevent drying. Place about a half-cup of apple mixture in center of phyllo, about one inch from the narrow end. Fold sides of phyllo toward the center, overlapping edges slightly. Roll up and place seam side down on a nonstick or ungreased baking sheet. Repeat with remaining phyllo sheets and apple mixture. Brush all tops with melted margarine or butter before baking.

Bake 30 to 35 minutes or until golden brown. Cool.

Makes 8 servings

NOTE: When baking with phyllo, I like to use butter instead of margarine because the finished product tastes much better (although it does have cholesterol, unlike the margarine version on which the Nutrition Facts are based). To lower your Facts and Exchanges, cut your portions in half.

NUTRITION FACTS: Serving size-1 Calories 241 Protein 3.7 g. Fiber 2.4 g. Carbohydrates 33 g. Sugars 17 g. Total Fat 11 g. Saturated Fat 1.5 g. Sodium 197 mg. Cholesterol 0 mg.

EXCHANGES: Bread .23 Fruit 1.3

Chocolate Roll-Ups

1 package of 8 refrigerated crescent rolls
2 ounces (2 squares) unsweetened baking chocolate
1 packet sugar substitute or 1 teaspoon granulated fructose
4 teaspoons all-fruit, seedless raspberry jam (no sugar added)

Preheat oven to 375°. Lightly oil a baking sheet or use a nonstick one.

Separate crescent rolls. With a rolling pin, roll out each piece of dough between two pieces of waxed paper to make them 50 percent larger. Set rolls aside.

Cut chocolate into small pieces. In a small ovenproof cup, combine chocolate, sugar substitute, and jam. Melt mixture together in a microwave oven set on high for 30 to 45 seconds, or melt over boiling water in the top of a small double boiler. Quickly stir together while hot. Use a table knife to spread a layer of chocolate on each roll. The chocolate can be difficult to spread. After spreading with the knife, you may have to pat and spread out some of it with your fingers. Roll up from the pointed end to the wide. Pinch each side to seal and place seam side down on baking sheet.

Bake for 15 minutes or until dark golden. Remove from oven. Cool for 10 minutes, then place roll-ups on a wire rack to finish cooling. When cooled, use a sharp knife to cut each one into 8 small pieces.

Makes 64 small pieces

NOTE: "Chocoholics" will savor the rich raspberry chocolate flavor in these delightful tiny treats. I think they are better than candy. These are a great way to satisfy your sweet tooth, remember that a little bit goes a long way.

NUTRITION FACTS: Serving size-1 Calories 19 Protein .47 g. Fiber .27 g. Carbohydrates 2 g. Sugars .18 g. Total Fat 1.1 g. Saturated Fat .66 g. Sodium 20.2 mg. Cholesterol 1.9 mg.

EXCHANGES: Bread .1 Fat .2

Fruit Jam Roll-Ups

1 package of 8 refrigerated crescent rolls
4 tablespoons apricot all-fruit jam, no sugar added
3 tablespoons finely chopped walnuts

Preheat oven to 375°. Lightly oil a baking sheet or use a nonstick one.

Separate crescent rolls. With a rolling pin, roll out each piece of dough between two pieces of waxed paper to make them 50 percent larger. Set rolls aside.

In a small bowl, warm the jam in a microwave oven set on high for 30 to 45 seconds, or heat in a small nonstick frying pan. On each roll, lightly spread the jam and sprinkle some nuts on top. Carefully roll up from the pointed end to the wide. Pinch each side to seal and place seam side down on baking sheet.

Bake for 15 minutes or until dark golden. Remove from oven. Cool for 10 minutes. Place roll-ups on a wire rack to finish cooling, or serve them warm. Use a sharp knife to cut each one into 8 small pieces.

Makes 64 small pieces

NOTE: These roll-ups are very tasty and just right for that "little something" you want to eat with your coffee, tea or milk. They make great snacks for children. Try different flavors of spreadable fruit each time you bake them. If you serve them whole, please remember to adjust your Facts and Exchanges by multiplying by eight.

NUTRITION FACTS: Serving size-1 Calories 17 Protein .34 g. Fiber .09 g. Carbohydrates 1.7 Sugars .60 g. Total Fat 1 g. Saturated Fat .22 g. Sodium 38 mg. Cholesterol .21 mg.

EXCHANGES: Bread .1 Fat .2

Cinnamon Tortilla Shells

3 large, fat-free flour tortillas
Pam butter flavor cooking spray
1 tablespoon cinnamon sugar made with Sweet 'n Low or granulated
  fructose

Spread each tortilla out on a bread board and spray evenly with Pam.
  Sprinkle evenly with cinnamon sugar. Slice into 4 quarters.
  Preheat oven to 350°. Oil spray 12 large muffin cups or use nonstick
pans. (You can also use small tart pans.) Drape each muffin cup or tart pan
with a piece of tortilla. Shape it so that it will hold a filling. Bake for 5 to 10
minutes, checking frequently. When crisp, remove from oven. Place each
shell on a wire rack and cool completely.

Makes 12

NOTE: Just before serving, fill with creamy custard or pudding, fruit, or
sugar-free, nonfat ice cream. Top with cinnamon sugar or serve plain. These
shells will keep for several days, but *never* fill them ahead of time because
they will get soggy. Eat immediately after filling.

NUTRITION FACTS: Serving size-1 Calories 46 Protein 1 g. Fiber .44 g.
Carbohydrates 8 g. Sugars .17 g. Total Fat 1 g. Saturated Fat .16 g.

EXCHANGES: Bread .53 Fat .09

Almond Chocolate Mousse

1 tablespoon or 1 envelope unflavored gelatin

1 1/2 cups skim or 1% (extra light) milk, divided

2 egg yolks

1/3 cup Sugar Twin or 5 tablespoons granulated fructose

1/3 cup unsweetened cocoa

1 teaspoon almond extract, or more to suit your taste

2 egg whites

1 teaspoon Sugar Twin or granulated fructose (optional)

In a small saucepan, combine gelatin and 1/2 cup of the milk. Let stand for 1 minute. Cook over medium heat, stirring constantly for one minute or until gelatin dissolves. Remove from heat.

Whisk together 1 cup milk, egg yolks, and 1/3 cup Sugar Twin. Add 1/3 of the yolk mixture and the cocoa to the saucepan. Beat or whisk vigorously until very smooth. Mix in the rest of the yolk mixture and cook over medium heat for 8 minutes, stirring constantly until slightly thickened. Because it is made with gelatin, it will not be as thick as regular pudding, but it will thicken as it chills. Remove from heat, stir in almond extract to taste, and chill for 20 minutes.

Beat egg whites in bowl until foamy. Gradually add 1 teaspoon Sugar Twin or fructose a little at a time, beating until stiff peaks form. Gradually add chilled chocolate mixture to egg whites. Fold in gently. Spoon into dessert dishes or leave in bowl. Chill 2 hours or longer. Cover with plastic wrap to prevent a skin from forming.

Serves 6

NUTRITIONAL FACTS: Serving Size-1 Calories 70.4 Protein 6 g. Fiber 1.43 g. Carbohydrates 7.3 g. Sugars 4.5 g. Total Fat 2.3 g. Saturated Fat .88 g. Sodium 92.7 mg. Cholesterol 72 mg.

EXCHANGES: Bread .1 Carbohydrates .1 Lean Meat .4 Milk .3 Fat .3

Apple-Banana Jumble

2/3 cup low-fat milk

1/3 cup low-fat ricotta cheese

1/4 cup egg substitute or 1 egg, beaten

1 teaspoon vanilla extract

1/8 teaspoon ground nutmeg

1/4 teaspoon ground cinnamon

1/4 cup golden raisins

3 small or 2 medium sweet apples, peeled, cored, and sliced

2 medium ripe bananas, cut into 1/2-inch slices

3 slices crustless white bread, broken into small pieces

Preheat oven to 375°. Butter the bottom and sides of a 9 x 9 x 2-inch oven-proof dish or similar pan.

In a large bowl, combine milk, ricotta cheese, egg substitute, vanilla, nutmeg, and cinnamon. Beat until foamy. Stir in raisins. Measure enough apples and bananas to equal 3 cups. Stir into milk mixture. Just before baking, add the pieces of bread to the mixture. Stir in lightly. Pour mixture into prepared baking dish and spread out evenly.

Bake for 40 minutes or until knife in center comes out clean. Do not let apples get mushy. Jumble should look lightly browned around the edges and top, but do not burn. Serve warm or cold. Cut into squares or spoon into dessert dishes.

12 servings

NOTE: Did you notice that this recipe is made without any sweetener at all? This is why you must use sweet apples (Golden Delicious or Fuji preferably) and ripe bananas. However, bananas should still be firm enough to slice. Don't you think that the apple-banana combination has a great taste? My family really enjoys this one!

NUTRITION FACTS: Serving size-1 Calories 81 Protein 2.8 g. Fiber 1.45 g. Carbohydrates 15.36 g. Sugars 9.48 g. Total Fat 1.27 g. Saturated Fat .55 g. Sodium 68.1 mg. Cholesterol 2.48 mg.

EXCHANGES: Bread .3 Lean Meat .2 Fruit .7 Milk .1 Fat .1

Apple Jean

1 1/2 cups whole milk
1 1/2 teaspoons vanilla extract
1/2 cup egg substitute or 2 eggs, lightly beaten
5 slices of crustless white bread
1 teaspoon cinnamon sugar (see page 7)
3 medium sweet apples, cored, peeled, and sliced thin
1/2 cup coarsely chopped walnuts
1/2 cup golden raisins
1 teaspoon ground cinnamon
1/2 teaspoon ground nutmeg

Pour milk into saucepan. Stir and heat to scald, but do not boil. Cool slightly. Mix in vanilla and egg substitute. Set custard aside.

Tear up 3 slices of the bread and layer on the bottom of a 9-inch glass or ceramic pie plate or a 9 x 9 x 2- inch square glass or ceramic dish. Sprinkle half of the cinnamon sugar over the bread. Layer half of the apple slices on top, spread out half of the walnuts and raisins on top of the apples, and sprinkle lightly with half of the cinnamon and nutmeg. Arrange another layer of apples and repeat as above with nuts, raisins, and spices. Ladle half the custard over the apples. Break the remaining bread over the top and sprinkle with the rest of the cinnamon sugar. Ladle the remaining custard on top, making sure that all ingredients are moistened.

Preheat oven to 350°. Bake for 50 minutes or until bread is brown and knife inserted in center comes out clean. Remove from oven and cool in the dish. This is wonderful when served slightly warm.

Serves 12

NUTRITION FACTS: Serving size-1 Calories 127 Protein 4.7 g. Fiber 2 g. Carbohydrates 19.3 g. Sugars 10.7 g. Total Fat 4 g. Saturated Fat .7 g. Sodium 100 mg. Cholesterol 0 mg.

EXCHANGES: Bread .4 Lean Meat .5 Fruit .7 Fat 1

Apple-Raisin Rice Pudding

2 cups cooked white rice (drain excess water)
3/4 cup chopped apples cooked with 20 golden raisins (drain excess juice)
3 tablespoons skim ricotta cheese
1 teaspoon ground cinnamon
2 cups low-fat or whole milk
3 teaspoons sugar substitute or 3 tablespoons granulated fructose
3/4 cup egg substitute or 3 eggs, lightly beaten
1 teaspoon vanilla extract
1/4 teaspoon ground nutmeg

Preheat oven to 350°. Butter an ovenproof baking dish.

In a medium bowl, combine the rice, apple-raisin mixture, ricotta cheese, and cinnamon. Scoop into the prepared dish.

Pour the milk into a saucepan, add sugar substitute, and scald. Do not boil. Set aside to cool. Stir in the egg substitute and vanilla. Gently ladle custard mixture into the baking dish containing the rice. Let the custard rest on top or mix it all together, depending on your preference. Sprinkle the nutmeg on top.

Place baking dish in a larger pan filled with 1 inch of water. Bake for 45 to 60 minutes. When knife inserted in center comes out clean, the custard has set and will set more as it cools. Remove from oven.

Serves 8

NOTE: Rice pudding can be served warm or cold. The choice is yours as to whether you wish to serve plain whipped cream or some other topping with it. Eat a much smaller portion if you add the extras. If you are on a diet, omit the toppings altogether. You can do without the extra calories. It may taste better with extras, but it's vital to have self control. I personally prefer to make this with eggs, but again, keep in mind that it changes the Facts and Exchanges and may not be the best choice for you, depending on your health.

NUTRITION FACTS: Serving size-1 Calories 134 Protein 6 g. Fiber .8 g. Carbohydrates 17 g. Sugars 7.8 g. Total Fat 4 g. Saturated Fat 1.5 g. Sodium 85 mg. Cholesterol 6.8 mg.

EXCHANGES: Bread .50 Lean Meat .50 Fruit .31 Milk .25 Fat .50

Cranberry-Raisin Rice and Cereal Pudding

2 cups cooked white rice

3 tablespoons cooked 6-grain cereal

25 golden raisins

15 dried cranberries

1 1/2 cups low-fat or whole milk

2 tablespoons granulated fructose or 5 packets of Sweet 'n Low

3/4 cup egg substitute or 3 eggs, lightly beaten

1 teaspoon vanilla extract

1 teaspoon ground cinnamon

1/4 teaspoon ground nutmeg

Preheat oven to 350°. Butter or oil spray an 8 x 8 x 2-inch baking dish or use a nonstick baking pan.

In a large bowl, mix together the cooked rice and cereal. Stir in the raisins and cranberries. Set aside.

In a bowl, mix together the milk, fructose, egg substitute, vanilla, and cinnamon. Pour into rice and cereal mixture. Mix thoroughly. Do a taste test. Add a little more sweetener if needed.

Pour the pudding mixture into the baking dish and sprinkle the nutmeg on top. Place dish in a larger pan containing an inch of water. Place in center of oven and bake for 45 to 60 minutes, or until knife inserted in center comes out clean. When set, remove from oven. Custard will set further as it cools. Serve warm or cold.

Serves 8

NUTRITION FACTS: Serving size-1 Calories 148 Protein 5.7 g. Fiber .74 g. Carbohydrates 23 g. Sugars 5.8 g. Total Fat 3.6 g. Saturated Fat 1 g. Sodium 68 mg. Cholesterol 3.8 mg.

EXCHANGES: Bread .87 Meat .38 Fruit .21 Milk .19 Fat .4

Custard Delight

1 1/2 cups nonfat milk
1 1/2 cups low-fat milk
1 tablespoon sugar substitute or 3 tablespoons granulated fructose
4 tablespoons no-sugar-added jam or jelly
1 cup egg substitute or 3 eggs, lightly beaten
2 teaspoons vanilla extract
1/2 teaspoon ground nutmeg

Preheat oven to 325°. Pour milk into a saucepan (preferably nonstick). Add sugar substitute. Stir and heat to scald, but do not boil. Set aside to cool slightly.

In a small nonstick frying pan, heat the jam, stirring constantly until melted. Coat a 4-cup ovenproof baking dish with the melted jam. (Or you can also use two 2-cup dishes.) Cool.

Pour egg substitute into the slightly cooled milk in the saucepan. Add the vanilla and stir to mix. When mixed, gently ladle into the baking dishes of your choice. Try not to disturb the coat of jam or jelly. Sprinkle the nutmeg evenly on top. (It will float.)

Place custard dish gently into a larger pan. Add one inch of water to the larger pan and bake for 1 hour or until knife inserted in center of custard comes out clean. Custard will set further as it cools. Remove from oven and cool thoroughly. Cover tightly and refrigerate for 4 hours or longer. The colder it is, the better it tastes. Loosen edges with a knife and invert on a serving plate. The colorful jam coating will be on top, and not only does this dish look good, it tastes great!

Makes 8 half-cup portions

NOTE: Always use seedless jams or jellies. To save time, you can spread the jam or jelly without heating. Try it both ways and pick the method you prefer. The flavor is your choice. I prefer raspberry, blackberry, peach, or apricot. You can use orange marmalade also. Because we cannot make creme caramel, which uses browned granulated sugar, these unique improvisions create delightful and delectable flavors.

NUTRITION FACTS: Serving size-1 Calories 126 Protein 7 g. Fiber .82 g. Carbohydrates 15 g. Sugars 7 g. Total Fat 6.5 g. Saturated Fat 2.8 g. Sodium 112 mg. Cholesterol 3 mg.

EXCHANGES: Bread .25 Lean Meat .50 Milk .42 Fat .68

Strawberry Bavarian Dessert

2 cups fresh strawberries
1 packet sugar substitute or 1 teaspoon granulated fructose
1 small package (2-cup size) sugar-free strawberry gelatin
1 tablespoon plain gelatin or 1 packet
2 tablespoons cold water
1 cup boiling water
2 cups ice cubes
1/8 cup whipping cream or heavy cream

Put aside 10 or 12 large strawberries. In a small bowl, cut and dice the rest of the berries. Mix in sugar substitute.

In a bowl (at least 5-cup size), mix the strawberry gelatin with the plain gelatin. Add cold water and stir to dissolve. Add boiling water and stir to dissolve completely. Add ice cubes and stir until gelatin begins to thicken. Lift out the unmelted cubes. Pour in the cream and whip until fluffy. Next, stir in the chopped strawberries and then top off with the fresh whole berries. If they are very large, cut them in half to decorate the top.

Place in the refrigerator for an hour or more and then serve in your favorite dessert dishes.

Serves 8

NOTE: This is a light, airy, yummy dessert that folks of all ages really enjoy. You can dress it up with beautiful molds or parfaits. Use your imagination, and be ready to listen to the call for seconds. If you have a large family, you had better double up on this one. It's super on a hot summer day, and very low in calories, carbohydrates, and sugar.

NUTRITION FACTS: Serving size-1 Calories 29 Protein 1.8 g. Fiber .93 g. Carbohydrates 3 g. Sugars 1.9 g. Total Fat 1.34 g. Sodium 33 mg. Cholesterol 4.3 mg.

EXCHANGES: Lean Meat .06 Fruit .23 Fat .26

Zesty Bread Pudding

3 tablespoons margarine or butter
1 cup low-fat or whole milk
1 cup heavy or whipping cream
2 teaspoons vanilla extract
1 tablespoon sugar substitute or 2 1/2 tablespoons granulated fructose
1 cup egg substitute or 4 eggs, lightly beaten
8 slices crustless white bread
4 slices crustless white bread, toasted
1 teaspoon cinnamon sugar (see page 7)
About 50 golden raisins
15 walnut halves, coarsely chopped
1 teaspoon thinly sliced and snipped or grated orange or lemon zest
Ground nutmeg

Preheat oven to 350°. Butter the bottom and sides of an ovenproof 8 1/2 x 4 1/2 x 2 1/2-inch loaf pan.

Melt margarine in a medium saucepan. Add milk, cream, vanilla, and sugar substitute. Scald, but do not boil. Remove from stove. When slightly cool, mix in egg substitute and set aside.

Cut all the bread into thin strips. Arrange a layer of untoasted bread on the bottom of the prepared pan. Use enough to cover the bottom. Sprinkle half of the cinnamon sugar over the bread. Evenly place some raisins, walnuts, and zest on top. Using toasted bread, do the same for the second layer. Cover these two layers with some of the custard liquid. Use toasted bread for the third layer. Place the rest of the raisins, walnuts, and zest on top. The last layer will be an arrangement of untoasted slices of bread. Pour the rest of the custard on top evenly so that all the bread is moistened. Lightly sprinkle nutmeg on top.

Before placing the pudding into the oven, place the baking dish in a larger pan that is one-third full of water. This will prevent the bread pudding from burning and help it retain moisture. Bake for 45 to 55 minutes or until knife inserted in center comes out clean. Crust on top should be golden brown.

Makes 8 servings

NOTE: For faster preparation, use 12 slices of untoasted bread with crusts removed. This dessert is equally good served warm or cold. You can add a sauce of your choice or a sugar-free topping. Of course, it tastes great without anything added as well. Enjoy!

NUTRITION FACTS: Serving size-1. Calories 436 Protein 11 g. Fiber 2 g. Carbohydrates 33 g. Sugars 9.5 g. Total Fat 29.6 g. Saturated Fat 9.6 g. Sodium 353 mg. Cholesterol I 45 mg.

EXCHANGES: Bread .75 Lean Meat .29 Fruit.50 Milk .30 Fat 2

INDEX